# Uncomplicated

*Ruth Teal*

# Uncomplicated

## *Silver Linings from the Heart*

TATE PUBLISHING
AND ENTERPRISES, LLC

*Uncomplicated*
Copyright © 2013 by Ruth Teal. All rights reserved.

No part of this publication may be reproduced, stored in a retrieval system or transmitted in any way by any means, electronic, mechanical, photocopy, recording or otherwise without the prior permission of the author except as provided by USA copyright law.

Scripture quotations are taken from the Holy Bible, New Living Translation, copyright ©1996. Used by permission of Tyndale House Publishers, Inc., Wheaton, Illinois 60189. All rights reserved.

The opinions expressed by the author are not necessarily those of Tate Publishing, LLC.

Published by Tate Publishing & Enterprises, LLC
127 E. Trade Center Terrace | Mustang, Oklahoma 73064 USA
1.888.361.9473 | www.tatepublishing.com

Tate Publishing is committed to excellence in the publishing industry. The company reflects the philosophy established by the founders, based on Psalm 68:11,

*"The Lord gave the word and great was the company of those who published it."*

Book design copyright © 2013 by Tate Publishing, LLC. All rights reserved.
*Cover design by Rtor Maghuyop*
*Interior design by Jomar Ouano*

Published in the United States of America

ISBN: 978-1-62510-965-1
Religion / Christian Life / Inspirational
12.11.26

# Dedication

*To my mom, my role model.*

*I love you.*

# Table of Contents

# Introduction

*Uncomplicated* follows *Silver Linings*, my first book, in the same on the go style. I see God's hand in everything I do. I don't believe in coincidence or karma, but in a Holy God who is sovereign and in control of all things, including my life. Jesus Christ is the light of my soul, my Savior, my all in all. He is the reason I do what I do. I walk in the direction of his will for my life, and he is ultimate.

I cherish my family. A big thanks to my oldest daughter, Tonya, for helping me with the titles for both of my books. A big thanks to my youngest, Erin, for supplying me with much of my writing material—my grandchildren, Addi and Blake. I thank God for my husband and sons-in-law. He has blessed me enormously with my wonderful family.

Enjoy reading *Uncomplicated, Silver Linings from the Heart*. I would love to hear from you on my website, www.ruthteal.com. Follow me on Facebook ~ Silver Linings.

Blessings,
Ruth

# The Nazarene

## Our Savior

This pondering doesn't begin with a personal story, but rather from a passage from the Scriptures.

> Just then, a woman who had suffered from bleeding for twelve years approached from behind and touched the tassel on his robe, for she said to herself, "If I can just touch his robe, I'll be made well!" But Jesus turned and saw her. "Have courage, daughter," he said. "Your faith has made you well." And the woman was made well from that moment.
>
> Matthew 9:20–22

As I meditated on this passage, so many things were popping into my mind. This nameless woman would have been rendered ceremonially unclean, thus banning her presence from the temple courts. She would have been very weak physically, unless they had iron pills in Jesus' day. From Mark 5:26, we can gather she was poor, having spent all her money on doctors; and yet was still sick. The reason Jesus healed her was because of her great faith. She knew that his power was so great, that one touch of his tassel would heal her. I believe she was content with her physical healing, but Jesus wanted her whole being healed. Even as she stayed behind him to touch the tassel, Jesus wanted her to know that he knew she was there. Mark 5:30–31 tells us that the crowds were so thick they were nearly crushing him, and yet he knew she was there.

Can you even begin to imagine what, for only that one instant, she saw as he looked into her eyes? My mind wanders to catch a glimpse in my imagination. I think in that instant, all shame fell away from being ceremonially unclean for twelve years. Jesus Christ knew who she was, and he esteemed her. In the same manner that she became physically healed and strong, I believe spiritually she was made just as strong. Then the icing on the cake, Jesus called her daughter! This man, the one who spoke with more wisdom than any she had ever heard, called her daughter! The one who could slip through a crowd, heal the lame, make the blind see, the deaf hear; this man whose authority was above all kings—he called her daughter! I think in that one instant as he looked into her eyes, she knew he was the Christ, the Son of the living God.

As you read the passage again from Matthew 9, read it out loud and fill in the blanks with your name and your own circumstance. Then believe, and hear Jesus say, "Have courage daughter, your faith has made you well!" (*Your name*) who had suffered (*your circumstance*) approached from behind and touched the tassel on his robe, for she said to herself, "If I can just touch his robe,

I'll be made well!" But Jesus turned and saw her. "Have courage, (*your name*)," He said. "Your faith has made you well." And (*your name*) was made well from that moment. Amen!

## Attributes of God

- He is the bright and morning star.
- He is Alpha and Omega.
- His mercy is unending.
- His grace is unfailing.
- He is my peace.
- He gives his angels charge over me.
- He is the lifter of my head.
- He is my all in all.
- He is ultimate.
- He is wisdom.
- He makes my cup to run over.
- Great is his faithfulness.

- He hides me in the shelter of his wings.

- He restores my soul.

- He never leaves me nor forsakes me.

- He can be trusted with… everything and everyone in my life, including my heart.

- In him, all things are created.

- God knows how many hairs are on my head, and still knows every time one falls out!

- He is forever and ever, amen.

- He has a perfect plan for my life, and when I mess that one up; he helps me with plan B.

- He never gives up on me.

- He had pity on me.

- He knew I would need a Savior.

- He provided Jesus, and the cross as propitiation for my sins.

- Jesus offered me life.

- I accepted.

- He is *my* Savior and Lord.

- I am, because He is.

- I love him with all my heart, because he first loved me.

> He himself is the propitiation for our sins, and not only for ours, but also for those of the whole world.
>
> 1 John 2:2

*A thought to ponder*: Have you asked him to be your Savior?

## Crushed Diamonds

Spring came, and our deck needed pressure washed and stained. My husband was dreading it because it is fairly large. To avoid having to do it again any sooner than possible, he spent hours researching stains to find the best one, that one that would actually stay on the wood for hopefully a very long time. He finally made his choice. It wasn't available for purchase within even two hours of us, so he had to do all his ordering on line. The magical stain that fit all of his criteria was a water-based epoxy formula. Gene had planned to spray it on with a new spray gun he had received as a gift, but the directions said it must be brushed on. So brush it he did, following the directions to the letter, hoping it would last for the ten years the website claimed.

As he began to work with it, it was clear why it had to be brushed. The stain was the consistency of water, and as the brush stroked it on, it pushed it into all the pores of the wood. The spraying would have just laid on top. After two and a half months of hard work, it was worth it. The deck had never been more beautiful. The morning after he had finished the last rail, I went out early to water the flowers and the dew was actually sitting on top of the wood, sparkling. It looked like someone had tossed crushed diamonds down the entire length of the rail. It was amazing. Even rain doesn't soak into the wood.

I pondered this as I was spending time taking care of the flowers. When we receive Jesus Christ as our personal Savior, we receive the Holy Spirit. He penetrates our being down to our soul.

> When you heard the message of truth, the gospel of your salvation, and when you believed in Him, you were also sealed with the promised Holy Spirit. He is the down payment of our inheritance, for the redemption of the possession, to the praise of His glory.
>
> Ephesians 1:13–14

*A thought to ponder*: The Holy Spirit lives with and in us (John 14:17), and abides forever with us (John 14:16). He gives us joy (1 Thess. 1:6), hope (Romans 15:13), imparts the love of God (Romans 5:3–5), teaches us (John 14:26), and testifies of Christ (John 15:26). He is poured out into every fiber of our soul. Just as the brushing motion of the stain application caused it to go deep within the fiber of the wood, so goes the Holy Spirit in our soul. The best thing is, unlike the promise of the ten-year lifetime of the stain, he is with us forever. Our human mind will never be able to understand how Jesus Christ, God, and the Holy Spirit are one, yet each operate individually, but glory to God! He has given us everything we need with the provision of the Holy Spirit, our forever "soul stain"! Hallelujah!

## Four Minutes

My husband has the Big Green Egg smoker. It is ten years old and needing a few parts replaced. It was becoming quite the challenge to find them. Gene finally located the nearest factory, which was only two hours away. He found out the time they closed, and knowing we were cutting it very close, we took off. We thought we would be about fifteen minutes early. As it happened, we arrived exactly four minutes late. They were closed. There was nothing to do. They were just closed. He couldn't pick up his order, and there was no one with whom to negotiate. There was absolutely nothing that could be done. We were just too late.

A few days later I was talking with a friend of mine, Kathleen, and she shared with me how in two seconds her life changed forever because of a back injury due to a fall.

My dad who was in excellent health died with no warning to any of us in one second.

I began pondering on this. How fleeting time is! Here today and gone tomorrow, as the old saying goes. Many people get to the end of their lives with many regrets of how they spent (or didn't spend) their time. No matter how much money one has, you can never get the time back. Better to fully live each day, and make each decision with this in mind.

One last very sobering thought in regards to time: at the end of each of our lives, and one day we will all die, we will stand before our Maker. Do you know beyond a shadow of a doubt that you will take residence in heaven at the end of your life? No one knows how much time on this earth we have, except our heavenly Father. One day he is returning!

> Then we who are still alive will be caught up together with them in the clouds to meet the Lord in the air and so we will always be with the Lord.
>
> 1 Thessalonians 4:17

> For you are saved by grace through faith, and this is not from yourselves; it is God's gift- not from works, so that no one can boast.
>
> Ephesians 2:8–9

Sister, at the end of your life—or if he returns before you die—there will be no time to *make things right with God.* When that instant comes, in the twinkling of an eye it's over. Too late to change anything, too late to make amends. If you have never put your faith in Jesus Christ, right now, as you are reading this, it isn't too late. It is absolutely amazing to me that our holy God, the one and only living God, made a way for us to live in heaven with him forever. He provided a perfect, holy, unblemished Lamb of God—Jesus Christ, to come to earth to provide redemption for our sins. Living a blameless, perfect life on this earth, fully God and fully man, he rose again three days after being crucified, taking on the sin of the entire world. By grace alone we put our faith in Jesus Christ as the one and only way to heaven. Then we will live with the creator of the universe forever.

*A thought to ponder*: Have I trusted Jesus Christ as my personal Savior?

## Ultimate

I am in a ministry called the Pink Apostles of Southern Illinois. This is a community women's ministry whose purpose is to bring the good news that Jesus Christ is Lord and to provide encouragement for our sisters in Christ to our neighboring towns. I am always searching for ways to reach more women while keeping my eyes open to any adjustments the Lord wants me to make in my schedule or life for him. The deepest desire I have is to follow him in the path he planned for me before I was ever born.

My team and I have been reading books like *Radical* by David Platt and *Crazy Love* by Francis Chan. The book I am currently reading is *Bonhoeffer: Pastor, Martyr, Prophet, Spy* by Eric Metaxas. Every time our team meets, the question comes up, "What does God want us to do with this?" These people gave up much, some all, making God ultimate in their life. The main takeaway from these is that as Americans, we have so distorted how God wants his children to live. The great American Dream isn't in the Bible at all. The way these people altered their lives for Jesus is so radical, they make us feel guilty. I just read through Acts and Romans, and these stories pale in comparison to Paul. The Bible is living and breathing, sharper than any two-edged sword. The Holy Spirit speaks to us through the Word, and we can't read it without it changing our lives. I pondered on the guilt Paul must have felt due to his persecution of Christians before he was one. Acts 22:20 tells us that he was even 'standing by and approving' when Stephen was being stoned and killed. When Paul realized who Jesus Christ was, he made a 360-degree adjustment in his life.

As I have struggled with the question, I feel I have finally arrived at the answer through the reading of the Word. It's what I knew all along. The answer lies in 1 Corinthians chapter 12. In verses 4–11, Paul is teaching about all the different gifts given, but given by the same Spirit. In verses 12–31 Paul teaches that just as the body has many parts, it is only one body- so also is Christ. He teaches that not one body part is more important than another, and if the parts were all the same, where would the body be? There are many parts, but one body. He finishes the chapter with "I will show you an even better way." We can't compare our life to anyone else's. If we all did the same thing, we will be one body part, instead of the whole body. To live out 1 Corinthians chapter 12 is to make Christ ultimate in each of our lives. On our own body, if one part of it is hurting, we will take care of it so it is well again. If we treat our spiritual body in the same way as our physical body, we will be living to "Love, the superior way."

*A thought to ponder*: Do I exist on this earth in this moment in time for my happiness and to collect all the 'stuff' I want, or am I here to further the kingdom of God, with my being here not about me at all, but to serve Christ by serving others?

## The Furnace

Our oldest daughter, Tonya, and son-in-law, Josh, purchased their first home in Catonsville, Maryland, a few years before they thought this would work out. Housing is quite expensive in the DC area. After the initial signing of the contract between buyer and seller, an inspection is scheduled. Among a few minor things was the furnace situation. Air does blow out of it, but instead of being good hot air, it is just lukewarm.

This sent my mind into an immediate pondering. Just as a furnace that blows warm air is of little use, as Christ's followers, when our walk with God is lukewarm, we are of little use to him.

> I know your works, that you are neither cold nor hot. I wish that you were cold or hot! So, because you are lukewarm, and neither hot nor cold, I am going to vomit you out of my mouth.
>
> Revelation 3:15–16

Being lukewarm is like sitting on a fence, not being able to decide. It's like picking 5 on a scale of 1 to 10. It's like not having an opinion at all; it's a total cop-out! When a person picks a 5, you have no more idea of what they think than if they didn't pick a number at all. When we are lukewarm, we can't take a stand for anything because a lukewarm heart and mind is complacent. Have you ever tried to have a conversation with someone on a topic they hadn't formed an opinion on? It's very difficult and turns into a one-sided speech instead of a conversation. It's time to know what we think and know what the Bible has to say about it. Having the mind of Christ, 1 Corinthians 2:16 says we can have a voice for him! The more we read the Word, the more we understand God's character and then we will know how to think!

*A thought to ponder*: Don't be afraid to speak up and voice your opinion!

## Check That off the List!

I was minding my own business, feeling pretty good about myself. After all, I hadn't committed any big sin lately. No, I was doing a fine job of living out this Christian life, if I do say so myself! Let's see. Did I spend time in prayer today? Check. Did I read my Bible today? Check. Actually, two checks on that one, because I also worked on a Bible study. So, double check! Did I do a thoughtful good deed for someone today? Hmm… Well, not exactly, but I *did* smile and spoke politely to everyone I came into contact with! So sure, check that one off too. Boy, I don't know about you, but I'm thinkin' I am doing quite all right!

Until… I was working on my computer, and you know when you are on a website filling out a form, and that little line is at the bottom that says, "Check here indicating that you have read this and agree to the terms and conditions." Ooops. The Holy Spirit brought to my attention that I always check that box but never read the terms and conditions. Well, that's not really a lie, is it? And then there's that little thing about always going just a little tiny bit over the speed limit. You know, not enough to get a ticket. I am such a busy person after all, and my time is very important to me. Well, that doesn't really matter, does it? There was the little incident of reading my Nook on the plane. You know when the stewardess says to turn off all electronic equipment? I knew she wasn't talking about my Nook because I had it on airplane mode. That is until she saw me reading it…

Are these things blatant sin? No. But is it really living a holy life? Peter says in 1 Peter 1:13–16,

> Therefore, get your minds ready for action, being self-disciplined, and set your hope completely on the grace to be brought to you

> at the revelation of Jesus Christ. As obedient children, do not be conformed to the desires of your former ignorance but, as the One who called you is holy, you also are to be holy in all your conduct; for it is written, "Be holy because I am holy."

We need to remember that someone is always watching us. Our life, the way we live it, is our testimony. 1 Thessalonians 5:22 says, "Stay away from every form of evil." We need to keep our actions pure so others will see Christ in us. The old adage "I can't hear what you're saying because your actions are yelling so loudly" is so true. We are truly a walking billboard. The question is, Who are we advertising for?

*A thought to ponder*: Are you abstaining from all appearances of evil?

## Without a Trace

Our friend John McPeek has been looking for his washer and dryer since the tornado hit his town a few months back. His house is still under reconstruction. He's hoping to be able to move back in another month. While much of his home was badly damaged, the missing washer and dryer have him puzzled. How does something so large vanish without a trace; and two somethings at that? John owns one of our favorite pizza hangouts in our town, Mackie's Pizza. When we pop into his restaurant to eat, he gives us the latest update, which is always that they have still not been found. He lives in town with lots of neighbors around too. It's not like his house was in the middle of a huge field. Right after the tornado had hit, his part of the town was really messed up, so I thought it's not a wonder. I figured they would turn up as the cleanup got under way. Now I'm thinking it's not going to happen, after this much time has passed. The entire thing has me wondering about them after all this time. I mean, seriously, how did they absolutely, completely, disappear without a trace?

So let's think about this through another lens. When I read my Bible, I read such wonderful truths. I read promises and stories that greatly impact me. I tell myself I will never forget them. The next day I can't remember what it was that I didn't want to forget. Unless I write down the verse or reference, I often can't find it again. It's simply lost. I think to myself how in the world can I not find it?

> This is the disciple who testifies to these things and who wrote them down. We know that his testimony is true. And there are also many other things that Jesus did, which, if they were written one by one, I suppose not even the world itself could contain the books that would be written.
>
> John 21:24–25

I am so thankful that John wrote down all of these things. I've often wondered about all the many things Jesus did on this earth that didn't get written down. It amazes me that the Bible has been preserved for all this time. Just a few hundred years ago, no one was even encouraged to read a Bible and almost no one owned one. Today it's not uncommon for a household to own many copies in several translations. I don't know how many copies are in our house. When we don't read it, it's like John McPeek not trying to find his washer and dryer. As we have untold treasure worth everything right under our noses through the scriptures, yet don't see it through neglecting to open up the book, I wonder if the washer and dryer were crushed under the large quantity of debris in the area? Well, John McPeek, I don't think we'll ever know!

*A thought to ponder*: Each day we can find a wonderful truth in the scripture. What have you found today?

## The Full Blingy Armor of God

When I read my Bible, sometimes I like to place what I read in perspective of how it fits into my life today. I thought this would be fun on the armor of God. I am in no way changing the words of the Bible! This really only happens in my mind, but I thought I would share it with you today. So what can I say, but "Welcome to my somewhat strange mind!" First let's look at what the scripts actually say.

> Put on the full armor of God so that you can stand against the tactics of the devil. For our battle is not against flesh and blood, but against the rulers, against the authorities, against the world powers of this darkness, against the

> spiritual forces of evil in the heavens. This is why you must take up the full armor of God, so that you may be able to resist in the evil day, and having prepared everything, to take your stand. Stand, therefore, with truth like a belt around your waist, righteousness like armor on your chest, and your feet sandaled with readiness for the gospel of peace. In every situation take the shield of faith, and with it you will be able to extinguish all the flaming arrows of the evil one. Take the helmet of salvation, and the sword of the Spirit, which is God's word.
>
> Ephesians 6:11–17

Now to put it into my application: I put on the full armor of God so I can stand against the tactics of the devil. My battle is in the realm of the unseen, not against people. I must take up the full armor of God so I can resist in this evil day. After having made preparations, I take my stand.

- My scarf I tie around my waist stands for truth.
- My necklace stands for righteousness.
- My blingy flip-flops stand for the gospel of peace.
- My purse represents my shield of faith.
- My salvation runs throughout my body from my hat to my toes.

- My Nook goes with me everywhere I go in my purse, on which I have three Bibles downloaded, which represent the sword of the Spirit.

*A thought to ponder*: So as I get dressed, I can remember my armor and the fight that I am in daily against the wiles of the devil. As I read the Word in the morning, tie on my scarf—sometimes to my waist, sometimes to my hat, and sometimes to my purse—clip on my necklace, throw my toes in my flip flops, grab my purse and my hat, I remember. I remember to stand, to stand on the name of the Lord Jesus Christ, my rock and my Savior.

## Old is New

Our grandkids think we are so cool because we have the fat movies. We have the big fat movies that their mother and Aunt Tonya watched when they were little girls. Among the favorites are *Paper Brigade*, *Honey, I Shrunk the Kids*, the *McGee and Me* series, and the *Secret Adventure* series starring character Drea Thomas. They don't have a machine to play the fat movies in at their house. When their mother comes in while we are enjoying one of the fat movies, she looks at us in disbelief. The picture is fuzzy (to say the least), the sound is a bit garbled, and it is just plain not right. We do have three Blu-ray players, but none of this for Addi and Blake. No, thank you, they will stick to the awesome coolness of the vintage VHS. It is so funny what little it takes to make them so happy. They will both sit forever and listen to stories of when their mommy was a little girl. Anything I can find that she played with or board games she had are always a hit. I have never had very many toys at my house for them because they were always much more interested in random things around the house. For Blake, that would include Papa's barn. I can keep them entertained for hours in the kitchen, letting them help me do anything with food. I have a few pieces of tiny Tupperware that both of the girls had for a play set, but Addi and Blake use them like cooking utensils. For the kids, the old stuff is more interesting than the new. For them, it hasn't gone out of style or out of date.

The Bible has also never gotten outdated. It is the only book, written over hundreds of years ago, that is still as current as the day it was written. It is our heritage, and it is our family. We cherish it as a precious heirloom, and God's written word.

> For you know that you were redeemed from your empty way of life inherited from the fathers, not with perishable things, like silver and gold, but with the precious blood of Christ, like that of a lamb without defect or blemish. He was destined before the foundation of the world, but was revealed at the end of the times for you who through Him are believers in God, who raised Him from the dead and gave Him glory, so that your faith and hope are in God.
>
> 1 Peter 1:18–21

*A thought to ponder*: Through Jesus, old is new. We have new life through Him! Our faith and hope are in God, the author and finisher of our faith. Our most ancient book, the Bible, is the best!

## Interstate 95

My daughter Tonya and son-in-law Josh love living in Baltimore County, Maryland. There are many attractions and opportunities we don't have here in Southern Illinois. Tonya loves her job. They've got good friends, bought a house, and are very settled in. Tonya lives eighteen miles from Montgomery College where she teaches, which is usually a near-hour drive each way. Interstate 95 runs the entire East Coast. As Tonya drives from Baltimore in the morning to the college in Silver Spring, Maryland, two blocks from D.C., and then back again in the evening, she's in the D.C. traffic each way. Too many drivers have the local highways clogged up, so there is no shortcut. Interstate 95 has many, many lanes going both directions. It narrows down to only six lanes sometimes. Pretty much every day she sees a wreck. She's only been rear-ended once. Josh hasn't at all yet. I pray for their safety daily. At least once a week, the traffic is stalled for no apparent reason, and she's stuck. No way to get out and no place to go if you could get out. This traffic thing is their only downside to the area. A person can get nowhere fast in that part of the country. There is no running out for a quick minute to grab something at the store. It is a maze, and with the amount of lanes and the speed the traffic is moving, if you don't know where you're going, you're in trouble.

While Tonya and Josh have to know the infrastructure to be able to maneuver about their daily tasks, we can lean on Christ to guide and direct us in our plans for this life. Proverbs 3:6 says, "Think about Him in all your ways, and He will guide you on the right paths." Psalm 32:8 says, "I will instruct you and show you the way to go; with My eye on you, I will give counsel." As a believer in Christ, our plans should be his plans. We are no longer in control of the direction our life is going. We need to ask him the direction he wants us to go, and as these verses show; he will guide us. We have as many choices in this life as the number of lanes and paths leading to and from Interstate 95. Most of us could pick from several and do well. But the question is which path is the one God is leading you to follow?

> The Lord is my shepherd; there is nothing I lack. He lets me lie down in green pastures; He leads me beside quiet waters. He renews my life; He leads me along the right paths for His name's sake. Even when I go through the darkest valley, I fear no danger, for You are with me all the days of my life, and I will dwell in the house of the Lord as long as I live.
>
> Psalm 23: 1–4, 6

*A thought to ponder*: Are you following God's path for your life, or your own?

# Majestic

## The Rescue

I typed the word "rescue" in my Bible software program. When the information loaded, it is in the text of the HCSV Bible 157 times. Our God knows how to rescue his people, and he's very good at it. Psalm 91:1 says, "The one who lives under the protection of the Most High dwells in the shadow of the Almighty." I can testify it's the best place to live.

My husband and I had an ongoing stressful situation for a long time. I did my best not to worry but pray instead. And pray I did! After weeks and months of praying what seemed like the same prayer over this particular matter, I began to wonder if God was tired of hearing it. I know I was tired of saying it. I completely trust God with every area of my life, even when it doesn't make sense or I don't like it. At some point, I stopped telling God each individual concern and instead switched to telling him I knew he knew everything going on with this situation. I told him I needed help with it and that I trusted him. This began a new prayer for this circumstance. With this matter, I simply said, "I trust you, God."

From time to time I have to remind myself that I don't need to tell God how to fix my life. He knows all things—past, present, and future. We can trust him with our life even when it looks like nothing is happening. He has many promises for his children, but they all come with a stipulation. The following verses are but a few examples of his faithfulness. Each one is contingent on loving him, fearing him, and/or keeping his commands. When we have given our heart to him and made him our Lord and Savior, we can completely trust what the Word of God says. We can trust Jesus Christ our Lord with everything.

> Your Father knows the things you need before you ask him.
>
> Mathew 6:8b

> Know that Yahweh your God is God, the faithful God who keeps his gracious covenant loyalty for a thousand generations with those who love him and keep his commands.
>
> Deuteronomy 7:9

> For as high as the heavens are above the earth, so great is his faithful love toward those who fear him.
>
> Psalm 103:11

> But it is written: What eye did not see and ear did not hear, and what never entered the human mind- God prepared this for those who love him.
>
> 1 Corinthians 2:9

> Now the eye of the Lord is on those who fear him- those who depend on his faithful love.
>
> Psalm 33:18

Horrible things still happen to Christians. I have no answers why, except that maybe God is trusting us to help another through the same dark water, the way he did for us.

> We know that all things work together for the good of those who love God: those who are called according to his purpose.
>
> Romans 8:28

> When I became embittered and my innermost being was wounded, I was stupid and didn't understand; I was an unthinking animal toward you. Yet I am always with you; you hold my right hand. You guide me with your counsel, and afterward you will take me up in glory. Who do I have in heaven but you? And I desire nothing on earth but you. My flesh and my

> heart may fail, but God is the strength of my heart, my portion forever. Those far from you will certainly perish; you destroy all who are unfaithful to you. But as for me, God's presence is my good. I have made the Lord God my refuge, so I can tell about all you do.
>
> Psalm 73:21–28

My daughter Erin said to me the other day, "Mom, isn't this a dream come true?" on the way the Lord took care of our situation. I told her it wasn't, because I hadn't even allowed myself to imagine in the farthest corners of my mind that God would do what he did. It was a rescue. God reached down and resolved this very stressful ongoing situation in a manner that I couldn't have even asked or imagined (Ephesians 3:20).

> If we are faithless, He remains faithful, for he cannot deny himself.
>
> 2 Timothy 2:13

> Now to the King eternal, immortal, invisible, the only God, be honor and glory forever and ever. Amen.
>
> 1 Timothy 1:17

*A thought to ponder*: What issue or circumstance am I dealing with right now that I need rescued from?

## Addi, Our Princess

Our little princess, Addisyn Lainee Blue, came into this world and had her royal court falling at her feet from the moment her lungs drew her first breath. Like all little girls, as she has grown, she is fascinated with all the stuff of fairytales. Her parents took her on family vacation to Disney World. She is still talking about all the princesses she got to meet and have her picture made with.

After this, Addi got a Barbie dollhouse as a Christmas gift, with lots of Barbie's to play with. She also received as a gift the entire set of Princesses in Barbie doll sizes. So 99 percent of the time when we play with her dollhouse, it is with the Princesses. She knows which one is which, even when she mixes up their clothes. I'm still getting Sleeping Beauty and Cinderella mixed up.

I sewed Addi a princess dress for her following birthday, which she usually has on her body at least once per day. It is purple, the color of royalty and her very favorite color. Rainbow-colored tulle adorns the skirt in a very full top layer. As she spins, the tulle shoulder scarves fly in the wind.

Girls of all ages, at one time or another, dream of being a princess one day, just like Addi. When you become a child of God—guess what! You are a princess. Our heavenly Father is the King of the entire universe. Your life today may not feel like you're royalty, but hang on! Your day is coming! The most magical life you can imagine can't begin to compare with the reality of what you'll have in heaven with Him. God doesn't just give you a room in the castle—you'll have an entire mansion!

> But you are a chosen race, a royal priesthood, a holy nation, a people for His possession, so that you may proclaim the praises of the One who called you out of darkness into His marvelous light. Once you were not a people, but now you are God's people; you had not received mercy, but now you have received mercy.
>
> I Peter 2:9–10

*A thought to ponder*: No matter what's going on throughout your day, remember you're God's princess! In heaven, every wrong will be righted, and you'll want for nothing! You'll be basking in the presence of God, walking on streets of gold, being cherished by the one and only true King! A true love story if ever there was one!

## A Walk through History

I was sitting at a dinner following Shelbyfest in Herman, Missouri. My husband has restored a 1966 Fastback Mustang, so we frequently hang out at this type of event. The speaker was talking about the history of Ford Motor Company: Ford's Performance Niche. He was here from Detroit and giving us all kinds of history, showing how the Ford Motor Company made its mark on American history and how they continued to come up with niche products that kept them at the top of their field. As fascinating as this is, my mind couldn't keep from wandering—and pondering.

As the speaker was walking through the life of Ford from conception through today, highlighting the amazing power motors and the like that had come along, I began to walk through the history of my own life in my mind. I was flipping through the years in my mental file of the amazing things Jesus Christ has performed throughout my lifetime to prove what an amazing, real, one of a kind God he is.

Just to highlight a few:

After a very difficult labor, when my second daughter Erin was born the Holy Spirit woke me up in the night to walk down the long hall of the hospital to look at her when I could not get myself to fall back asleep. So with my C-section incision, I got out of the bed to make my way down to her room to find her lying on her side, blue, totally strangled, needing to be suctioned. Another minute or two more and she would have been gone from of us. I have been beholden to him every day of her life that he let her stay here with us. I can't imagine our family without her shiny, joyful brightness, our son-in-law, or our two precious grandchildren.

I am reminded of when my husband's optometrist found on a routine eye exam a tumor in his right eye. We went to his appointment with the head oncology eye surgeon at St. Louis Barnes hospital one month later to be told they could find nothing in his eye and didn't know why he was there, although we had the films showing the tumor.

My mind wanders to when our firstborn daughter, Tonya, was driving home on Interstate 57 during her second year of college in a horrible rain storm when we got the phone call that her car had hydroplaned, going into an uncontrollable spin. Her car finally stopped spinning when it ran into a semi truck, sending the car to the side of the road where she landed unharmed. She was only inches from hitting the gas tank of the truck. The driver was praying that he wouldn't run over her.

My God has proven himself over and over and over in my own personal life that his name is Faithful and True. My mind could wander on page after page. These are but a few of the reasons he holds my heart. He has shown himself over and over to be all that he says he is in his Word. I don't believe in coincidences but in God-ordained appointments. Even if you have been a person who until now hasn't given God the credit or even thought about him being responsible for the small and large incredible things that just happen to have happened in your life, now you can even begin to journal and record all of these amazing life events, thanking the One who has been seeing you through. What about the things that have or are happening in your life that don't look like blessings, but are in fact hardships in one way or another? I have those in my life too, but what I know is that God is faithful. We don't have to know the rest of the story. Some things in our life are a result of poor decisions, while others happen by nothing we have caused. What I know is that I can trust my God with everything, with every problem in my life, with my children, my grandchildren, my husband, and my entire family. He is faithful, and he is worthy of our praise! Amen and hallelujah!

> Let me experience Your faithful love in the morning, for I trust in you. Reveal to me the way I should go because I long for you.
>
> Psalm 143:8

*A thought to ponder*: Keep a journal of all the areas of your life God has shown his majesty. When you are going through a difficult situation, it is a great faith booster to be able to read it, reminding yourself that he is able and willing to care for you!

## 360 Degrees

I joined a women's gym called Great Shapes in a nearby town. My body was going downhill fast, and I thought I should do something about it before there was no return! I had injured my back the winter before and then most recently my knee. My entire body had gotten so stiff, and I figured these things would continue to happen if I didn't do something about it. I attended the yoga class to loosen up and then a strength-training class. The room the strength-training class was held in has mirrors around each wall. While little, tiny teacher Christina was lifting weights larger than her head, I was struggling to keep up with five- and ten-pound weights. While the class was quite difficult, she made it fun while we were all sweating and groaning. Before I went, I knew I needed to shed a few pounds.

After going to class after class and catching 360 degree glimpses of myself from time to time, I realized I needed to shed more than just a few. Doing a quick final check in my wardrobe mirror just before running out of my house wasn't the reality check of the 360 degree angle. After seeing this image time after time and having it seared in my mind, I realized it was time to really work on this area of my life—my sugar addiction. I had been trying to get serious about this, because my mom has diabetes. I simply couldn't quite get a handle on it. It wasn't until after I had the reality check on a regular basis I couldn't get away from, that 360 degree view, that I started losing weight. I didn't think it was really that bad. The mirrors showed me the truth—the cold, hard truth. After a few months, my husband asked me if I was having fun at the gym. I told him I wouldn't exactly call it fun, but that it felt really good to be taking care of myself. I also could never have put myself through the torture Christina put me through by myself. And all along, she was there, in the front, with that big smile on her beautiful little face.

This is why God left us with his word, the Bible. We look at ourselves and think we are pretty good. We think we are all right because we didn't murder anyone, we didn't steal, we didn't do anything really bad. Until we read in the Bible that the smallest, tiniest sin in our eyes is as wicked to God as the biggest sin we can possible think of, like murder. Until we read the Bible what truth is, we don't know what it is. It is in our 360 degree mirror, the one we can't ignore once our eyes have been opened.

When we have given our heart to Jesus and we place ourselves on a regular basis in front of the 360 degree mirror he left us with, we have to do something about the truth that we read. As we read the Bible, the Holy Spirit convicts our heart of things in our life we need to get rid of, and this is for our benefit. Sometimes we are convicted of something we need to add.

> This is eternal life: that they may know You, the only true God, and the One you have sent—Jesus Christ.
>
> John 17:3

> In the beginning was the Word, and the Word was with God, and the Word was God. He was with God in the beginning. All things were created through Him, and apart from Him not one thing was created that has been created. Life was in Him, and that life was the light of men. That light shines in the darkness, yet the darkness did not overcome it.
>
> John 1:1–5

> The Word became flesh and took up residence among us. We observed His glory, the glory as the One and Only Son from the Father, full of grace and truth.
>
> John 1:14

> Indeed, we have all received grace after grace from His fullness, for although the law was given through Moses, grace and truth came through Jesus Christ.
>
> John 1:16

*A thought to ponder*: What new truth has reading the Bible revealed to you today?

## The Jail Door

Three-year-old Blake was playing at our new McDonald's play land and went exploring outside of the structure. He discovered the very interestingly very narrow door in the side for the employees to get behind for repairs and cleaning. After trying his best to enter through the door and not being able to open it, he asked me if it was a jail door. While I thought this was hilarious, it *is* made out of black bars and had a lock on it. Since Blake's mind is at all times thinking of pirates, guns, and swordfights, I can see how this thought entered his little mind. I thought it was funny because you could plainly see through the door that no prisoners were on the other side. We had also recently watched the *Swiss Family Robinso*n from the Disney Vault. This concept of a jail door got my mind to wondering *How many jail doors do we lock ourselves behind of our own making?*

One could clearly see through this fascinating door at the McDonald's play land from either side. An employee in possession of the key could enter or exit at free will. The only reason a person wouldn't be able to get out of this jail is if the key was lost after entering. Then by yelling for help, another employee would come with another key and let the person out. We lock ourselves into all types of jails by not obeying the rules God left us in his Word. Sin will hold you much longer than you ever intended to stay, and you'll pay much more than you ever expected to pay. While we are being held behind these jail doors that we have built for ourselves, all we have to do is "yell" to God by repenting, and he will unlock our jail door and set us free!

> Hallelujah! My soul, praise the Lord. I will praise the Lord all my life; I will sing to the Lord as long as I live. Do not trust in nobles, in man, who cannot save. When his breath leaves him, he returns to the ground; on that day his plans die. Happy is the one whose help is the God of Jacob, whose hope is in the Lord his God, the Maker of heaven and earth, the sea and everything in them. He remains faithful forever, executing justice for the exploited and giving food to the hungry. The Lord frees prisoners. The Lord opens the eyes of the blind. The Lord raises up those who are oppressed. The Lord loves the righteous. The Lord protects foreigners and helps the fatherless and the widow, but He frustrates the ways of the wicked. The Lord reigns forever; Zion, your God reigns for all generations. Hallelujah!
>
> Psalm 146

*A thought to ponder*: Are you in a jail of your own making right now? Request the key from your Father. He will set you free! Amen!

## The Heritage Trail

My husband and I decided to take a three-day weekend trip to celebrate our thirty-second wedding anniversary. We drove to Northern Indiana to drive the Elkhart County Heritage Trail. It wove through miles of Amish country and small towns. The way the county set up this trail was really unique. You go to the visitor center and pick up a CD package of directions along with a map. All you have to do is pop in the first CD and off you go! We had never done anything like it before. The CD tells you which direction to take, where to turn, and interesting places a person may like to stop and explore. The map wasn't even necessary, except to make control freaks (hmmmm…) feel like they are still in control. As long as we followed the instructions on the CD, we didn't get lost. Every now and then, we didn't listen closely enough and got off track. We would then have to retrace our steps and start over.

Pondering, as I do, this got stuck in the back of my brain. Wow! How like our Christian walk is the heritage trail in Elkhart County, Indiana! The Lord God gave us an instruction manual for every area of our life, the Word of God, our Holy Bible. In it are the words of life, words of encouragement, and how to handle ourselves and make decisions both big and small. When we follow it, we find our way through this life, seeing sights and wonders we never knew existed. When we follow God's direction through the leading of the Holy Spirit and let go of the reigns of our life, letting him completely guide us, we are living our best life. It doesn't even matter if things don't always look so rosy. When he is in control of our life, our decisions, we don't have to try to figure things out. He knows what tomorrow holds, not us. He knows what he is doing, and all we have to do is follow the guidebook—not looking with our eyes at situations we're in, but completely trusting him. Do we ever get off course? You bet! The longer you live this faith walk, the quicker you realize you veered off and the sooner you backtrack, getting back on course.

How many times do we mess things up because we stopped following the manual? Too many to count, no doubt. God, in his ever-present mercy and grace, always is ready to take us back, forgive our bad choices, and then—of all things—help us out of the mess we got ourselves into! Unbelievable! He never washes his hands of us. Hallelujah! He is the lover of my soul, my ever present prince of peace, my savior! If you don't know him in this way, you're only one prayer away from his mercy and salvation.

> Trust in the Lord with all your heart, and do not rely on your own understanding; think about Him in all your ways, and He will guide you on the right paths.
>
> Proverbs 3:5–6

*A thought to ponder*: Are you traveling on the perfect path God designed for your life?

## Wedding Cakes

We used a salt chlorinator on our above-ground pool. It was great. In the beginning, it was a bit expensive to buy, but very cheap to run for the life of the pool. I liked it because it didn't make your skin itch or fade the liner. When you were done swimming, it was so mild you didn't even need to take a shower to get the chemicals off your skin. The bad thing about it was it shortened the life of the pool, a lot. In fact, the store we purchased that pool from didn't sell another salt generator with an above-ground pool. It rusted the entire thing. We now have the second pool put in, without a salt generator. We had steps called wedding cakes in the first one, which we are also using in the second, instead of a ladder. They actually do look just like a wedding cake. I was washing it before placing it into the new pool. It is one plastic type unit, biggest at the bottom and gradually getting smaller as you get to the top. Gene places sand bags inside the unit under the bottom step to weight it down so it won't float. Algae had grown inside the steps, where, while it was immersed into the water, it couldn't be seen or reached to clean. All the outside of the unit was fine, because the movement of the water in combination with the sun and chemicals kept the algae off. I was scrubbing away to get all the crud completely off the inside before we tossed it in, and every time I would flip it upright, I would find more. It was hidden down into the farthest nooks and crannies. The contraption is big and cumbersome to move around, even on the deck. Finally, Gene or I couldn't find any more of the crud, and at last, the thing was clean.

> This, then, is the judgment: The light has come into the world, and people loved darkness rather than the light because their deeds were evil. For everyone who practices wicked things hates the light and avoids it, so that his deeds may not be exposed. But anyone who lives by the truth comes to the light, so that his works may be shown to be accomplished by God.
>
> John 3:19–21

*A thought to ponder*: The algae, like sin, likes to be hidden in the dark, avoiding the light. Is there any hidden sin in the nooks and crannies of your heart that you need to let God clean up?

## The Storage Box

Gene bought a huge plastic storage box eight years ago to store pool toys and maintenance paraphernalia on the deck. It has worked well. Everything is in one place and always neat. The plastic screws broke off the two heavy lids last summer. All summer I was fighting with those cumbersome lids to keep them on just so, so they would stay on. Anytime the wind picked up, they would get blown off. This spring, I talked him into replacing it. He didn't want to, because all he needed were replacement plastic screws. He looked online several times last summer but could never find the company to buy them. We brought a new box home from Menards for $220. He opened the box, took out the bag of screws, and they fit. He googled the company that manufactured the new box and was able to purchase the screws for twenty-three dollars. After taping the entire cardboard box back together, we took the new one back to the store. He was a very happy camper!

All things on this earth eventually break. Parts decompose, break down, and wear out. Our bodies do the same. Today we can get replacement parts for lots of pieces on our body. Doctors perform organ transplants today on a daily basis. The plastic surgery industry is at an all-time high. Youth (or looking youthful) is attainable at a high price. Until we get to heaven, these bodies are going to gradually wear out from the time we are born until we die.

> For we know that if our temporary, earthly dwelling is destroyed, we have a building from God, an eternal dwelling in the heavens, not made with hands. Indeed, we groan in this body, desiring to put on our dwelling from heaven, since, when we are clothed, we will not be found naked. Indeed, we groan while we are in this tent, burdened as we are, because we do not want to be unclothed but clothed, so that mortality may be swallowed up by life. And the

> One who prepared us for this very purpose is God, who gave us the Spirit as a down payment.
>
> 2 Corinthians 5:1–5

*A thought to ponder*: Let your mind wander to that day in the future when we are living in heaven with God—always youthful, no pain of any kind (emotional or physical), beautifully clothed, and beautiful. There are colors in heaven that we have never seen nor could be described here. No need for plastic surgeons there! Nothing to wear out or fade! Living in the glory of the Son forevermore, truly reflecting his radiance!

## Patience is a Virtue

My daughter Erin and I live in the same town. My other daughter, Tonya, lives on the other side of the country. Erin prepared a very elegant Mother's Day brunch for me and her two grandmothers. As soon as little Blake ate his last bite of food, which was about fifteen minutes after we arrived, he was ready for me to play with him. I told him when his great-grandmas left, that we would play. After he asked me several more times within a few minutes, I promised him I would stay a very long time after the great-grandmas left, so he didn't need to worry. I told Blake he and Nana would play a really long time. As three-year-olds' timelines go, that worked for about thirty more minutes.

About two and a half hours after we arrived, Great-grandma Donna left. Now he just had to wait for Great-grandma Kay to go. Grandma Kay was now being entertained by five-year-old Addi. Addi was giving her lots of art gifts from the large collection she had created. After listening to Addi read one of her learning books to her, she was going to be on her way. Blake couldn't take it any longer. He went and found Grandma Kay's shoes, running them to her. He said, "Grandma Kay, can you go now?" At this point, we were all in tears laughing. He loves his great-grandmas, but he really, really wanted to play with Nana.

Blake is three. That entire thing was funny. It isn't funny when adults behave this way. Are we really any more patient than Blake? We ask God for him to show us his will for us, but do we actually wait for his answer? Sometimes he tells us our answer right away but asks us to wait. The time is not yet. Do we wait? Sometimes he wants us to be trained or learn something to be able to complete our next task. Do we take the time to do this? Do we try to manipulate situations to make them happen when we want them to? As mature adult Christians, we must practice patience through self control. As we grow, we should be increasing in our spiritual maturity level. The only way to grow in patience is to practice it. Each time it will get easier. I promise!

> Therefore, since we also have such a large cloud of witnesses surrounding us, let us lay aside every weight and the sin that so easily ensnares us. Let us run with endurance the race that lies

> before us, keeping our eyes on Jesus, the source and perfecter of our faith, who for the joy that lay before Him endured a cross and despised the shame and has sat down at the right hand of God's throne.
>
> Hebrews 12:1

*A thought to ponder*: Is there an area of your life you need to ask God to help you be patient in?

## Restored

We have a beautiful maple tree in our backyard. It is directly behind our deck where the pool is. An inland hurricane hit our area three years ago. If you know I live in Southern Illinois, you are thinking the word "hurricane" doesn't fit into our vocabulary here. That's what all of us thought, too. We aren't aware of this happening before, but anyway, it did happen three years ago on May 8. It looked like a tornado had come through, and that word is definitely a part of our vocabulary. When it was all said and done, we were told it was an inland hurricane. The property where we live wasn't damaged much. From where we live down to Kentucky and Tennessee, there was much damage overall.

I'm not making light of the horrific amount of damage by talking about my maple tree, but rather it reminds me of the beautiful restoration our Lord has in store for those who trust in him. We had planted this tree many years ago as a small sapling. The storm removed the center branches of this once-beautiful tree. It became, within minutes, rather unsightly. It's the tree I see when I look out my kitchen and dining room windows and while we are on the deck. With the budding of the leaves this spring, we noticed that the center was completely filled back in. The branches are all full and bushy, with no holes at all. Gene and I didn't think it would ever be restored to its original state.

Our lives can be ugly and a mess from doing it on our own. When we haven't given our heart to Christ, it has an unfilled hole in it. Like the tree, our center is empty and void of life. On our own, we have no way to rejuvenate it. Only through giving our life to Christ, relinquishing all control of it, will our center be filled.

> When goodness and love for man appeared from God our Savior, He saved us—not by works of righteousness that we had done, but according to His mercy, through the washing of regeneration and renewal by the Holy Spirit. This Spirit He poured out on us abundantly through Jesus Christ our Savior, so that having been justified by His grace, we may become heirs with the hope of eternal life.
>
> Titus 3:4–7

*A thought to ponder*: Have you given up complete reign on your life, submitting to Jesus Christ as your Savior and Lord?

## iPod

Gene gave me a pink iPod for Christmas several years ago. I am crazy about it. The next year he gave me a Bose speaker for it, now even more awesome. Before the speaker, I tried to carry it around the house all day wearing the earphones. It was difficult, and the battery ran down fast. My car has an outlet for the iPod. It keeps it charged, so I can listen no matter how long I'm driving. I used it this way until I got my Droid smartphone, which allowed me to load my iTunes library. The car can stream my music off the phone so I can now leave the iPod at home on the speaker. I can listen to dozens of CDs on one tiny device. I even have some audiobooks on it. I used to have a tote bag full of my CDs in my trunk, with a visor clip full of the ones I was currently listening to. Let's not forget the large portable CD device we used to carry around. Technology is great. I don't understand how it works. All I know is what used to fit in a large tote bag now fits in a two-by-four-inch flat device that's smaller than my cell phone.

I often declare that I can't memorize verses any more or that it's getting harder to remember things I have poked into my brain. I think what's really happened is that we all have *so* much information stuffed into our brains that we're on information overload. Scientists say all of us only use a very small portion of our brain. The way God created our brain is unbelievably incredible. It is slightly bigger than an iPod but holds far larger quantities of memory. Psalm 139:14 says, "I will praise You, because

I have been remarkably and wonderfully made. Your works are wonderful, and I know this very well."

*A thought to ponder*: Thinking of the large tote bag I used to hold my many CDs, I wonder how many very, very large tote bags it would take to hold all the information we have stored in our brains! Thank God for making our minds so remarkable and wonderful!

## Junk to Treasure

My good friend Gail is a junker. She buys people's junk they are tired of and resells it. She is very good at her business. Gail is very creative, full of energy, and she knows what will sell. The best thing, she loves it. Junk is her passion. She's done many different things through the years, but she always comes back to her junk. The most interesting part of the whole thing to me is when she puts it out to sell, it doesn't look like junk anymore. She cleans it up, tweaks it here and there, and ends up with an eye-appealing item that doesn't sit around long. I wouldn't give a second glance to most of the stuff she starts out with. It would end up in my trash. She has a gift for seeing through things. What I see with my eye in front of me, she sees as it will be after she has done her magic to it. Some of the items require lots of time, but those usually bring her the biggest turnover. She puts a little love into the remaking and a little creativity, and it always pays off for her. Gail calls herself a junker, but I call Gail a treasure seeker.

Isn't this just like our God? When we look like junk, smell like junk, and act like junk, God sees us as we will look after he's cleaned us up. He can't clean us up until we come to him though. We have to come to him just as we are, looking like something ready for the trash. God looks at us through the blood of Jesus as beautiful and redeemed. Once we fall into his hands, we come out on the other side looking like treasure. Ezekiel 16:14 says, "Your fame spread among the nations because of your beauty, for it was perfect through My splendor, which I had bestowed on you. This is the declaration of the Lord God."

*A thought to ponder*: See yourself through the eyes of Christ as the beautiful treasure you are!

# Woven

## Disillusioned

My husband and I had taken a trip to Branson. I had to make adjustments to our travel plans only a week and a half prior to our departure, which left us with only one resort with an opening. Instead of the one-bedroom-apartment size I had previously booked, our only option was a suite. I made Gene aware of this before I finalized it and got his okay. We just needed to get away for a few days, and we didn't care where the location was. We arrived, checked in, and got our bags up to the room number they gave us. To our surprise, it was the one-bedroom-apartment size. I didn't give it a second thought because we are automatically upgraded if possible. We dropped everything on the coffee table and plopped down on the sofa to rest a minute before we started settling in. Unexpectedly, company arrived about three minutes later! They even had their own door key that fit into our lock. As they came walking through the door, I began to feel like Goldilocks. Upon calling the front desk, it was determined that we had been given the wrong room. We retrieved the correct room key, collected our bags once again, rode the elevator back up, and entered the correct room. It was exactly what we had been promised—a suite. Now Gene wasn't happy and began to complain about the room. He was content to have the suite before we had walked into the much-bigger apartment. I told him it was exactly what I was promised on the phone at the time I booked it, and the other one was never ours to begin with. He continued to compare it to the larger one, and I continued to remind him nothing had been taken from us. What we were staying in was exactly what we had been promised. We even got a goody basket of treats as an apology for the mix up.

I actually thought this entire episode was particularly funny. I began pondering on all the situations that happen to us by none other than a blessing from God. We begin to think we somehow deserve to have this thing that we neither asked for nor worked for. We have many promises available to us in the Bible, but most are not automatic. Most of them are contingent on something we have to do on the front end.

Definition of "promise"—declaration by one person to another that something will or will not be done, giving the person to whom it is made the right to expect the performance of whatever has been specified.

In James 4:7–10, we have several promises. We are promised that the devil will flee from us, but first we must resist him. We are promised that God will draw near to us, but only after we draw near to him. God says *he* will exalt us, but only after we humble ourselves.

John 20:31 says, "But these are written so that you may believe Jesus is the Messiah, the Son of God, and by believing you may have life in His name."

You see that eternal life is not automatic just because you attend church every Sunday or were born in the USA or your parents are Christ followers. Each individual must make their own decision to believe and accept the Lord as their personal Savior. When we belong to Christ, we have many, many promises given to us in the Word of God. God gave it to us that we can live with hope and security in this life. The only thing we can count on today is Christ. By believing in his name, we not only have life everlasting, but (1) peace like a river, (2) a Father who is able to do above and beyond all that we ask or imagine, (3) resting in God's righteous right hand, (4) living under the protection of the Most high, and (5) dwelling in the shadow of the Almighty.

*A thought to ponder*: You will not be disillusioned when you put your trust in Christ.

## The Crocs

I love to buy my grandkids Croc shoes. We now have a tradition of shopping for new Crocs in the early spring, and I always stuff a pair in their Christmas stockings. We go to the Great Outdoors store in a nearby town to try them on and pick out their new pair. While they have lots of styles and colors in stock, every time—and I do mean every single time—the only pair on their shelf that fits Blake Lewis is green. The last time this happened, I told him I could order a different color on the computer. In the excitement of walking out of the store with a new pair that fit, he chose to walk out with the oh-so-familiar green ones. Most days, the Crocs are all he wants to wear. His mother Erin loves them because no matter how much mud and crud he walks through, she can just rinse them off and they are clean. Blake loves them because they are comfy, quick, and easy to put on. He doesn't care at all that they always look the same.

Just like Blake's Crocs always being green, our God never changes. The God of the Bible is always the same. From Genesis 1 to Revelation 22, he is the same. Our God is impartial, full of grace, and available for redemption to all who ask. We can fully trust him with our lives even when we can't see him working. The most amazing thing about God is that he provided a way for us to live with him throughout all eternity in heaven. This amazing God of ours loves us so much that he sent his only Son, the perfect Lamb of God, to be our Savior. The only thing he requires of us is to believe that through that son, Jesus Christ, is the one and only way to heaven. Then we have to ask him. Salvation isn't automatic. After believing, we have to ask him. That's it. When we have made him our Savior and Lord, we can rest on all the promises we read in the Bible. Just as Blake's Crocs have always been green, God's promises are always true. His Word is always true. He is Yes and Amen!

> Trust in Him at all times, you people; pour out your hearts before Him. God is our refuge.
>
> Psalm 62:8

> Now the eye of the Lord is on those who fear Him- those who depend on His faithful love

> to deliver them from death and to keep them alive in famine. We wait for Yahweh; He is our help and shield. For our hearts rejoice in Him because we trust in His holy name. May your faithful love rest on us, Yahweh, for we put our hope in You.
>
> Psalm 33:18–22

## The Gentleman

Our son-in-law started teaching our grandson about manners when he turned two years old. Jacob has been teaching little Blake that he is to be courteous of his mother and sister, because he is a man and they are ladies. They hadn't told me this, and it took me awhile to catch on to what he was doing. This little guy would run to beat Addi and I to a door to open it for us. I would run after Blake to help him, with Addi yelling to me that Daddy had taught him to be a gentleman. It was a very hard thing to just stand there, letting this little guy pull and tug on a big heavy door five times larger than him. It would be all I could do to not help him. Also humorous was watching Blake jump on the Tahoe running board to tug and pull on the driver's door to open it for his mother. Blake's face beamed when he would accomplish one of these feats.

Jacob was already instilling in Blake at this very young age that he was a man and he was to be respectful of women, regardless of their age. I must say I have never had a door opened for me as much in my entire life as I have by my little grandson. Sister, about now you may be feeling a little sorry for yourself, wishing you had a gentleman like this in your life. Perhaps you walk through this life never knowing what it's like to be treated with respect or feeling cherished by your father or husband. As women, whether single or married, we all long to be treated as a princess. We want to feel like we are special to at least one other person on this earth. I must say there is a little girl somewhere on this planet that is going to live her adult life feeling like a princess by Prince Blake.

Before you fall into a pit of absolute despair, I have great news for you. As a child of the King, you are a princess! Your heavenly Father, the King of the universe, cherishes you. He created you, and he loves you beyond measure. He brings us to repentance so we can rid our lives of sin, not to bring us shame. No matter what we've ever done, as soon as we confess it to him, with immeasurable grace he opens his arms to us with total love and forgiveness. Unlike humans do oftentimes, he never brings it up to us again.

He is truly the perfect gentleman. Giving Christ total reign of our lives, he guides us in the perfect way for our journey through this life. I didn't say easy way, but the perfect way. Just as a diamond has to go through fire to be beautiful, we also have to go through some heat for our lives to be used by God.

No matter what anyone has ever said to you, the only truth is what your heavenly Father has to say about you. According to Psalms 103:3, he crowns you with love and compassion; in Psalm 107:8, his love is unfailing. According to Ephesians 3:20, he is able to do immeasurably more than all we could ask or imagine, according to his power that is at work within us. In Romans 3:24, we know that we are justified freely by his grace through the redemption that came by Christ Jesus. Matthew 28:20 tells us he will be with us always to the very end of the age. Romans 8:38–39 tells us that neither death nor life, neither angels nor demons, neither the present nor the future nor any powers, neither height nor depth nor anything else in all creation will be able to separate us from the love of God that is in Christ Jesus our Lord.

*A thought to ponder*: Sister, you are highly esteemed, respected, and loved by your heavenly father, the King!

## A Tribute to Mom

I am so blessed to still have my mom here with me on this earth. My dad went to heaven six years ago, and I still miss and love him with all my heart. But God has been so good to me that Mom's still here, though she's getting close to eighty years old. As I meander through my life in my mind, so many things cross through of life's blessings through Mom. The biggest blessing of all was to be raised in a Christian home, with parents who loved the Lord. My mom was and is always an encourager. Any idea I ever in my life ran by her to see what she thought was always answered with an "I'm sure you can do it, and you'd be great at it too." I was never afraid to try anything I was pulled towards through her encouragement. Mom has always been there when I needed a travel buddy or someone to de-stress with and escape for a "fun day." When Gene and I were newlyweds (over thirty-three years ago), she would *never* listen to any complaints I had about him. She taught me early on to work things out between us. Without saying it in words, she told me she loved Gene as much as me and was going to be as loyal to him as me. No favorites, even with her son in law. Mom taught me how to do life by watching hers. I watched her walk her talk, and it was genuine. She witnesses to everyone who gets in her space. She was an awesome grandma to my girls when they were growing up, and they have many great memories of being with her. In a nutshell, Mom taught me how to live life, how to love God, how to be a wife, and how to parent my daughters. And I don't think she ever realized that she was doing all of this. She was just being my mother.

> Honor your father and your mother so that you may have a long life in the land that the Lord your God is giving you.
>
> Exodus 20:12

> For God said: Honor your father and your mother; and, The one who speaks evil of father or mother must be put to death.
>
> Matthew 15:4

> A mother is one who can take the place of all others, but whose place no one else can take. (Irish proverb)

*A thought to ponder*: Take a moment to thank God for your mother, and if you didn't have one or she wasn't the role model mine was, thank him for who he put in your life to fill in the gap. If she's still living, write her a note (yes, the old-fashion type, with a stamp and everything!) to tell her how much you appreciate her.

## Blake

My three-year-old grandson, Blake, likes to talk. A lot! Like he never, ever stops. We often have to hold up a stop-sign hand to let his sister, Addi, get a word in edgewise! We can't figure out who he got it from (oopsie…me). I would just like to insert right about now that God made me this way, so it's okay, right? Well, as you can guess, he and Addi have their Nana wrapped around her little finger about a million times. Blake and Addi, as I write this, are my only grandkids or, as I like to call them, my precious angels. My mom bought a wooden sign for them to give me for my birthday that says "I can at Nana's." I told her it should say "I can *with* Nana." It's a good thing their parents discipline them well, or they would be ruined for sure.

Okay, so on with the pondering! As I was saying, Blake likes to talk a lot. Lately one of the things he says to me often is "Nan, do you nememer (remember) when…?" Often he's talking about something that happened as soon as the day before. It is so cute. When he starts the conversation, you think he's digging way back into the past. However, for a three-year-old, I guess yesterday is a long time ago. So I go *talking* down memory lane with him. He also loves to hear stories about his mother when she was a little girl. When I tell him a new story about her he hadn't heard yet, we will rediscuss that half a dozen times at least as we are "nememering."

God wrote his story for us to remember, so many stories to build our faith, to see his glory, and as the ultimate guide book for our life. We can read about all the stories of God bringing the Israelites out of Egypt, remembering that he still delivers us from bondage today. We read in the New Testament how Jesus treated people, and we then remember when we are interacting with others the right way to treat them. When wrong has been done to us, we remember from God's Word that he highly esteems us and calls us his daughters. Yes, the entire story of God was written that by reading it, we will truly know him, his character, and who he is. The most important thing to remember is because of his great love for us, his Son died a horrific death on a cross two thousand years ago so we would have a Savior worthy to redeem us, and redeem us he did!

> For God loved the world in this way: He gave His One and Only Son, so that everyone who believes in Him will not perish but have eternal life.
>
> John 3:16

*A thought to ponder*: Am I reading my Bible often enough to be able to actually remember?

## The Body

My husband, Gene, is a commercial plumber. He literally nearly cut off the end of his finger working on a job at our local Target store. He put his finger in the pipe cutter instead of the pipe. He wasn't going to go to the emergency room until convinced by fellow workers. It was so bad they made an appointment for him to see an orthopedic surgeon five days from the accident. If it wasn't reattaching by then, the surgeon was going to remove it that day. (I know, really gross…) In his thirty-five-year career, Gene had never had an accident like this. He still doesn't know how it happened. Thank the Lord, it healed up and he didn't have to lose it.

Two days later, he was making some repairs on our deck and had tools lying everywhere. He stepped on his saber saw and cut open the end of his big toe. Another accident he never has. We were able to bandage this injury up at home. So he now has his right hand and his left foot bummed up. He was really having an off week! You wouldn't think the end of two appendages would slow you down. He's a working machine, and he kept going but had to be extra cautious with how he was moving. Two tiny, tiny areas on his entire body effected how he made every movement. I think he would have been glad if he could have left those two parts at home until they were healed up.

> For as the body is one and has many parts, and all the parts of that body, though many, are

one body—so also is Christ. For we were all baptized by one Spirit into one body—whether Jews or Greeks, whether slaves or free—and we were all made to drink of one Spirit. So the body is not one part but many. If the foot should say "Because I'm not a hand, I don't belong to the body," in spite of this, it still belongs to the body. And if the ear should say, "Because I'm not an eye, I don't belong to the body," in spite of this it still belongs to the body. If the whole body were an eye, where would the hearing be? If the whole body were an ear, where would the sense of smell be? But now God has placed each one of the parts in one body just as He wanted. And if they were all the same part, where would the body be? Now there are many parts, yet one body. So the eye cannot say to the hand, "I don't need you!" Or again, the head can't say to the feet, "I don't need you!" But even more, those parts of the body that seem to be weaker are necessary. And those parts of the body that we think to be less honorable, we clothe these with greater honor, and our unpresentable parts have a better presentation. But our presentable parts have no need of clothing. Instead, God has put the body together, giving greater honor to the less honorable, so that there would be no division in the body, but that the members would have the same concern for each other.

1 Corinthians 12:12–25

Just as Gene couldn't leave his toe or finger behind, we can't leave our sisters and brothers in the Lord behind. The physical body doesn't operate correctly without all the members, in the same way our spiritual body can't.

*A thought to ponder*: Which member are you in the body of Christ?

## The Tractor

I use my husband's tractor about twice per year. In the fall to clean up the flowerbeds, and in the spring to clean them up again, getting them ready for the spring/ summer. This pattern has been going on a long time, at least ten years. I always tell him when I'm going to use it. I know absolutely nothing about the way it runs, so this way I know it's okay for me to use it. This spring, when I was ready to do my major cleaning up, I went through this same pattern. Gene was leaving for work, and I asked him if the tractor was good for me to use that day. He said yes, so off on it I went. We have woods surrounding all of our property. As I break off all the dead stuff, I throw it in the tractor bucket. When it's full, I drive it down to the woods and dump it off. This is repeated many times until they are clean. On my last trek down, the tractor was slowing down on me as I was coming back up the hill. I couldn't figure out on earth why. I looked around under the steering wheel for gauges and couldn't really make heads or tails of it. I then wondered if I had ran out of gas, something I had never thought about before. I had never put gas in it. I turned the key, and it ran. That's all I knew about that. I jumped off and walked back up to the house.

When my husband came home he wanted to know why I left the tractor out in the yard. I told him it stopped running, so I couldn't put it back. He asked me if it ran out of gas, and I told him I had no idea. He asked me if I checked the gas gauge, and I told him there wasn't one to check. He wasn't looking very happy with me. He said I ran it out of gas, and he would now have to take it into the tractor shop (what???? tractor shop??? Gene always tinkered with it himself) and have the motor rebuilt. Something about priming the motor. I told him I didn't know what he was talking about, and I wasn't taking the blame for whatever he was saying because I told him I was going to use it and he said okay. I told him if there was something that serious about driving it that he should have told me a long time ago. I'm not an irresponsible person, and had he shown me, I would have watched for that situation.

So the story goes on. I told him that maybe he should go and get some gas and try to start it before he got all in a huff. He said there was no way it was going to start, and he didn't feel like pulling it onto the trailer yet. So it sat. Then it rained, and he couldn't do it. So it sat. It sat, and it sat, and it sat. It sat until I was getting really tired of looking at it in the yard. Anytime I would bring up the getting-some-gas-and-trying-it idea, he would just get all mad again. Finally, he decided to deal with it. He did get the gas and try to start it, and yes, you guessed it, it started right up! He spent so much energy being frustrated and mad when all along it was fine.

How many times do we do this with situations in our life that frustrate us? We stew and stress and worry and fret, when all along all we had to do was turn it over to the Lord. We often think there isn't a simple answer to our problem, but it usually is simple. It's just not what we want to do. We can find the answer to every situation in black and white in the Bible, but we often want a different answer. When we do finally turn it over to God and do that thing he is showing us, it's never as bad as we imagined. It's, for me, always a relief. The more we do this, the quicker we release it to him, until we finally wise up and admit it's always the best thing to go with God's advice at the front end. He does always have our best in mind.

> Therefore let us approach the throne of grace with boldness, so that we may receive mercy and find grace to help us at the proper time.
>
> Hebrews 4:16

> Now to Him who is able to do above and beyond all that we ask or think according to the power that works in us- to Him be glory in the church and in Christ Jesus to all generations, forever and ever. Amen
>
> Ephesians 3:20–21

*A thought to ponder*: What situation is in your life right now that you need to turn over to God? Peace returns the instant you do!

## Social Networking

Technology has turned the world upside down, in a good way, to keep connected today! It's mind boggling how Facebook has brought so many people who live physically far apart so close together. I could never figure out how to get pictures from my regular camera onto the site, and I used to only get on about once a month to check out what was going on. Introducing…the smartphone! After this arrived on the scene, it was a whole new world. I now can easily upload pictures and reply to posts. Yes, it's a whole new world. Each decade brings changes that bring the world together tighter and closer than ever. We have Skype and Tango, free video chatting through the World Wide Web. My daughter who lives fourteen and a half hours from me can see changes I make to our home or anything else I want to show her instantly through Tango. *Almost* as good as her being here. We can virtually keep up with anything in the world today by using Google. Every news channel has a Facebook site too, so you can find out new local news the minute it happens. Foreign countries don't seem so foreign anymore. We used to have to purchase expensive picture books if we wanted to see what another country looked like. Not now…Google strikes again! People can talk in real time to each other from anywhere in the world—strangers or friends—on the computer, for free I might add. People who look different from us because they live half a world away don't seem to look so different anymore, because of seeing them so regularly. Ethnic barriers are breaking down quickly due to this familiarity.

Just as the world doesn't seem like such a big place anymore, and the lines that divide all of us are growing very fuzzy and dimming, in Christ we have no lines. Christ died for all, period. The only line separating one from another in the heavenly realm is who believes and who doesn't.

> Do not lie to one another, since you have put off the old man with his practices and have put on the new man, who is being renewed in knowledge according to the image of his Creator. Here there is not Greek and Jew, circumcision and uncircumcision, barbarian, Scythian, slave and free; but Christ is all and in all.
>
> Colossians 3:9–11

*A thought to ponder*: For fun, try this for awhile: look at everyone not based on what their race or ethnic background is or even the country they live in, but do they believe in Christ or not?

## The New Frontier

I marvel at my seventy-seven-year-old mother. She cracks me up. She has yet again taught me some valuable information about a website we both use. We were both frustrated with a particular matter, and she is the one who solved it. She bought the first iPad in our entire family, completely on her own I might add. She is simply fearless! If she can't figure something out, instead of getting embarrassed, she makes a phone call to ask someone. She keeps digging around until she has her answer. She is a role model for younger women in many areas of life. When my dad died suddenly over six years ago, instead of allowing herself to drift off in a crippling state of depression, she made herself get up every morning and go on with her life. She and my dad did *everything* together and were very close. I watched her lean on the Lord, drawing from his strength until she had her own back. We are so much a product of our upbringing. A very true quote from an old favorite movie *Hope Floats* is

> "Childhood is what you spend the rest of your life trying to overcome. That's what Momma always says. She says that beginnings are scary, endings are usually sad, but it's the middle that counts the most. Try to remember that when you find yourself at a new beginning. Just give hope a chance to float up."

I have often said it was so easy for me to trust and believe in God because of the father I was given on this earth and the unconditional love I received from both of my parents. I have also wondered many times, why me? Why did God choose to allow me to have it so easy and wonderful? I will never know that answer, but I am so thankful to him. The blessings he has given me on this earth are unending and blessings that can't be bought with money. As you are reading this, if you didn't have it so easy, there is hope. According to the wisdom of man, it's nearly impossible to escape your upbringing. In another favorite movie, *The Blind Side*, Michael is asked how he did it: how he really got away from the poverty he was born into and the life that is so common that goes along with it— drugs, alcohol, dropped out of school. His answer was he simply closed his eyes to the bad. I have yet another answer, an even better one than that. No one but God can truly renew us. No one but God can completely heal us from past wounds. Next to salvation, I think it is the most amazing thing he does for us. When we allow him to, he 100 percent heals, restores, and makes us whole. It is a miracle. There is no therapist, psychiatrist, or drug that can do this for us. Not only does he do all of this, he redeems our past wounds by allowing us to be a blessing to others through what we went through.

> He *renews* my life; He leads me along the right paths for His name's sake.
>
> Psalm 23:3

> But those who trust in the Lord will *renew* their strength; they will soar on wings like eagles; they will run and not grow weary; they will walk and not faint.
>
> Isaiah 40:31

> Do not be conformed to this age, but be transformed by the *renewing* of your mind, so that you may discern what is the good, pleasing, and perfect will of God.
>
> Romans 12:2

> Therefore we do not give up; even though our outer person is being destroyed, our inner person is being *renewed* day by day.
>
> 2 Corinthians 4:16

*A thought to ponder*: Is there an area of your life you need to give to God, allowing him to make you whole? He not only heals you, but will redeem the wound that was inflicted on you if you let him!

# A Peak behind the Curtain

## The White Stone

When my daughter was pregnant, a very popular topic of discussion was the baby's name. Napkins made good doodle pads at restaurants, baby name books were always handy, and different spellings were considered. Except for decorating the nursery, it was at the top of the list, always! When my brother Dave got a new puppy, it took him and his wife, Stachia, a week to pick out his name. Isaac Newton was carefully selected for the little white ball of fur.

Names are very important to us. It makes us feel that we're important to other people when they remember our name. Our God is so detailed and cares about our universe to the point that "He brings out the starry host by number; he calls all of them by name. Because of his great power and strength, not one of them is missing" (Isaiah 40:26). Again in Psalm 147:4, the Bible says, "He counts the number of the stars; he gives names to all of them." Our God loves us so much that in Matthew 10:30, the Bible tells us that "even the hairs of your head have all been counted." I used to work as a cosmetologist, and the number of hairs on your head changes hourly.

We have nothing in us that makes us worthy to live in heaven with Jesus at the end of this life. We were born into sin. We needed a Redeemer and Savior who could be our atonement. Jesus Christ came to this earth, born of a virgin, living a blameless and pure life. John 20:31 says that "these are written so that you may believe that Jesus is the Messiah, the son of God, and by believing you may have life in his name." Jesus Christ is the only living God, the only way for us to get to heaven. We will live for all eternity in heaven with Christ when we completely believe that he is the only name by which we are saved. God loved us so much that he provided his Son as our Savior. Second Timothy 2:19 says the Lord "knows those who are his." We can know we belong to him by reading 1 John 5:13, which says "I have written these things to you who believe in the name of the son of God, so that you may know that you have eternal life."

Sister, God not only knew what your name was before you were even conceived, but he is also giving those who are his a new name! Revelation 2:17 says, "We will be given a white stone, and on the stone a new name is inscribed that no one knows except the one who receives it." Can you even imagine trying to name every child of God who ever lived and who will ever live? There is debate among the scholars if our name written in the Book of Life is our current name or our new name. I've been pondering on when we actually receive the white stone; perhaps it will be handed to us as we walk through those pearly gates. Perhaps when we see Jesus face-to-face for the very first time he'll hand the stone to us then. I think it will be written in Hebrew or Greek, and we will be able to understand it. Every time Jesus renamed a disciple or patriarch in the Bible, it was for a reason and the name meant something. I think our new name will have a reason behind it and not be haphazardly picked. What an amazing God we serve, that he cares this much about us. He is crazy about you!

*A thought to ponder*: What new name would best describe you?

## The Song Singer

When my friend's son Jared was small, he would add ribbon to the end of empty wrapping-paper rolls, place it around his neck, and pretend it was an instrument. He called this creation his song singer. I can picture in my mind this small boy playing the life out of this instrument! The Bible has a lot to say about music, singing, and playing instruments. Isaiah 55:12 says, "The mountains and the hills will break into singing before you, and all the trees of the field will clap their hands." God created us to worship him. Our lives are to bring him glory, with the entire Bible written to point us to Christ.

This little boy grew to love Jesus and made him his Savior. When he was sixteen, he had a tragic automobile accident, leaving a huge unfillable hole in the hearts of his parents and sister. On this earth, we will never be able to understand why things like this happen. I like to imagine him in heaven, playing with all the passion he did as a small boy, on a stringed instrument of solid gold made exclusively for him by our Lord. He is singing praises to our God in a language none of us have ever heard on this earth, with a voice that would win him a big-time music contract here.

> Rejoice in the Lord, you righteous ones; praise from the upright is beautiful. Praise the Lord with the lyre; make music to Him with a ten stringed harp. Sing a new song to Him, play skillfully on the strings, with a joyful shout.
>
> Psalm 33:1–3

*A thought to ponder*: Jared's life impacted every teenager he knew at his high school for Jesus. We won't know until we join him just how many came to know Christ because of the way he lived his life. Are you living your life in wild abandon before the God of the universe, allowing all you come into contact with to see him through you?

## Sunscreen

I had purchased a convertible, which is the first time I had ever ridden in one. It was a retractable hard top, and the convertible part had nothing to do with why I bought it. I just liked the car and that was how the hard tops came. From the very first time I dropped the top, I was hooked! You are probably beginning to connect the sunscreen title. I have never cared about or made a point to be in the sun or get a tan. I am not saying I don't like to have a tan. My tan comes out of a can. I have a fair complexion and am pretty careful about using sunscreen, trying to avoid skin cancer.

When spring came and I started dropping the top, I kept getting burned on the top of my ears (short haircut). From habit, I had put the sunscreen on every other part of my body. I was amazed every night, when my ears would start itching from being burned, at this amazing stuff in a tube! All the rest of my exposed skin was just fine, not even pink.

Just as this invisible layer of protection shields and protects our skin from the harmful sun's rays, God protects our life when we put our faith in him.

> But let all who take refuge in You rejoice; let them shout for joy forever. May You shelter them, and may those who love Your name boast about You.
>
> Psalm 5:11

> The Lord is my rock, my fortress and my deliverer, my God, my mountain where I seek refuge, my shield and the horn of my salvation, my stronghold.
>
> Psalm 18:2

> He alone is my rock and my salvation, my stronghold; I will never be shaken.
>
> Psalm 62:2

> But the Lord is faithful, He will strengthen and guard you from the evil one.
>
> 2 Thessalonians 3:3

God is invisible to us, yet very real. When we choose to put our faith in Christ and live our lives the way the Bible tells us to, we very much have protection in all areas of our lives. Just as we have to put on sunscreen every day to protect us for that day, we have to put on our spiritual armor daily.

> Put on the full armor of God so that you can take a stand against the tactics of the devil. For our battle is not against flesh and blood, but against the rulers, against the authorities, against the world powers of this darkness, against the spiritual forces of evil in the heavens. This is why you must take up the full armor of God, so that you may be able to resist in the evil day, and having prepared everything, to take your stand. Stand, therefore, with truth like a belt around your waist, righteousness like armor on your chest, and with your feet sandaled with readiness for the gospel of peace. In every situation take the shield of faith, and with it you will be able to extinguish all the flaming arrows of the evil one. Take the helmet of salvation, and the sword of the Spirit, which is God's word. Pray at all times in the Spirit with every prayer and request, and stay alert in

> this with all perseverance and intercession for all the saints.
>
> Ephesians 6:11–18

*A thought to ponder*: Let's live our lives with fearless abandon; putting our faith in the One who created us and wants only the best for us. You are free to dance the dance of your life in His arms, in His protection and faithful love.

## The Sour Grape

I was eating a bunch of grapes. They were big and juicy and sweet. I had three left, so I popped one off and puckered up! Boy, was that one sour! It was shocking because the others were so sweet and all from the exact same piece of the twig.

As I pondered on this, I am reminded of the parable of the vine and the branches (John 15:1–8). Just as the sour grape turned the bunch of grapes from being remarkable to being mediocre, I am so glad the Father prunes off the branches that are dead. Dead branches bog down a beautiful vine, and dead branches on our spiritual vine bog down our Christ walk. I think that as long as we live, we will have "dead stuff" in our lives that Christ needs to clean up. There are so many issues that we can find temporary, worldly, fleshly fixes, like even determination to prune our own selves, which we don't have the capability to do. When we give these things to

Christ and allow him to deal with these issues, he prunes them in just the right way, and our vine remains healthy and well.

> I am the true vine, and my Father is the vineyard keeper. Every branch in me that does not produce fruit He removes, and he prunes every branch that produces fruit so that it will produce more fruit. You are already clean because of the word I have spoken to you. Remain in Me, and I in you. Just as a branch is unable to produce fruit by itself unless it remains on the vine, so neither can you unless you remain in Me. I am the vine, you are the branches. The one who remains in me and I in him produces much fruit, because you can do nothing without me. If anyone does not remain in me, he is thrown aside like a branch and he withers. They gather them, throw them into the fire, and they are burned. If you remain in Me and My words remain in you, ask whatever you want and it will be done for you. My Father is glorified by this: that you produce much fruit and prove to be my disciples.
>
> John 15:1–8

*A thought to ponder*: What do you need to let God prune from your branches today?

## The New Normal

Jamie Lee Curtis stars in an Activia yogurt commercial. The makers of Activia claim that by eating their product on a regular basis, it will renew your digestive system—thus, your new normal. All of this with the simple addition of a yogurt product! Amazing! There are lots of other women in the commercial claiming to have their new normal.

I began pondering how Christ has given my mind a new normal. When we put our faith in Christ through reading of the Scriptures, we begin to think differently. When we think differently, we act differently. After we've been walking with him for a time—and for me it's been a very long time—I've definitely gotten a new normal. This is all to his glory and to our benefit! Knowing God is sovereign and that all things work to the good of those who love him allow us able to accept difficult situations much easier. We know he is working in every aspect of our lives even when we don't understand the why.

> Do not be conformed to this age, but be transformed by the renewing of your mind, so that you may discern what is the good, pleasing, and perfect will of God.
>
> Romans 12:2

*A thought to ponder*: In what way has your *new-normal* thinking made your life easier to maneuver?

## Living for an Audience of One

Now that I have turned fifty years old, I know what I like. During my young adult years, I hated having to do a self quiz or answering questions about myself for a couple's game at a Sunday-school party. My husband and I had taken classes at church on personalities, and I would always have to ask him what my answers were. I always thought it very odd that someone else seemed to know me better than I knew myself.

Now that I have lived approximately two-thirds of my life, I know the answers. After working through numerous Bible studies most of my adult life, listening to many wonderful sermons, reading through the Scriptures for myself, and spending untold hours in prayer, I know what's important to me, and what is not. I finally realized that I didn't have to impress anyone or live up to anyone else's expectations except the Lord's. And now it doesn't even bother me. I live for an audience of one. Jesus has my best interest at heart, is compassionate, and full of mercy and grace. I can rest assured that if I am pleasing him, I am also treating others in the best way I can. Because I have given my life to him and am a dedicated Christ follower, we are yoked together, Jesus and I. I stay on his path for my life, and there I have freedom to be the person he has designed me to be. I love him, and him alone I want to please and obey. After all, he gave up everything for me to be able to live with him for all of eternity in heaven. I have everything to gain by following him.

> Love is patient; love is kind. Love does not envy; is not boastful; is not conceited; does not act improperly; it is not selfish; is not provoked; does not keep a record of wrongs; finds no joy in unrighteousness, but rejoices in the truth; bears all things, believes all things, hopes all things, endures all things. Now these three remain: faith, hope, and love. But the greatest of these is love.
>
> 1 Corinthians 13:4–7, 13

*A thought to ponder*: You can trust him with your heart. He will never betray you, mislead you, use you, lie to you, or treat you with disrespect. He will never belittle you or make you feel shame.

## Poolside

Gene and I have been cleaning up outside getting ready for the summer. We love being out on our deck and relaxing. He had some repairs to make on the deck, and I had a lot of work getting the flowerbeds ready for the season. Once the beginning work is done, it's simple and only needs small amounts of time to keep it up. The problem I have with the hard work that requires lots of time getting it ready is that I can't take the heat unless I'm wet, in the shade, or air-conditioning. Exerting a lot of energy with the temperature cranked way up does me in fast. To keep from getting sick, I run the hose on me a lot. I still don't feel good, but it works. It allows me to keep working until I can get finished. The flowers are so beautiful. It is worth every sick-feeling minute to be able to enjoy them the rest of the summer.

When I have something to get done, I want to get on with it until I'm finished. I have a hard time stopping even to rest. Once I start a project, I dig in with both hands and nearly kill myself to finish before stopping. This is how my personality works. I have to fight it all the time. With the help of my husband and practice that comes with age, sometimes I can defeat the urge and stop to rest. If it's a project that simply cannot no matter what be completed in one day, I have to accept it and roll with it. When I do, I'm much calmer and peaceful inside, not to mention it keeps my blood pressure low, when I accept that it's going to take some time to finish.

> There is an occasion for everything, and a time for every activity under heaven: a time to give birth and a time to die; a time to plant and a time to uproot; a time to kill and a time to heal; a time to tear down and a time to build; a time to weep and a time to laugh; a time to mourn and a time to dance; a time to throw stones and a time to gather stones; a time to embrace and a time to avoid embracing; a time to search and a time to count as lost; a time to keep and a time to throw away; a time to tear and a time to sew; a time to be silent and a time to speak; a time to love and a time to hate; a time for war and a time for peace. What does the worker gain

> from his struggles? I have seen the task that God has given people to keep them occupied. He has made everything appropriate in its time. He has also put eternity in their hearts, but man cannot discover the work God has done from beginning to end. I know that there is nothing better for them than to rejoice and enjoy the good life. It is also the gift of God whenever anyone eats, drinks, and enjoys all his efforts. I know that all God does will last forever; there is no adding to it or taking from it. God works so that people will be in awe of Him. Whatever is, has already been, and whatever will be, already is. God repeats what has passed.
>
> Ecclesiastes 3:1–15

As Solomon said, it is a gift from God that we can enjoy our efforts. I stand in awe of God as I gaze at his beautiful creation. That I can relax, peaceful inside, enjoying the flowers and all that summer brings is his gift.

*A thought to ponder*: Recreation and enjoyment of our labor is a gift from God. Remember to thank him for this too!

## Blessings Disappear

My mother-in-law, Donna Teal, said something very interesting to me. She had seen a saying that said, "Imagine all the things you are thankful for. Which of these did you thank God for? Now imagine all the things you didn't thank him for disappearing." Ouch! These are but a few:

- © **T**he joy knowing my Savior gives me
- © **H**ome and family
- © **A**nswered prayer
- © **N**ever having to worry, but giving everything to God through prayer
- © **K**nowing I belong to Christ
- © **F**or precious moments in time that fill up my memory bank
- © **U**mbrellas and Christ's **u**nfailing love
- © **L**iving in the USA, where I can worship Jesus freely!

I have been keeping a journal this year only of things that happen that I'm thankful for. Nothing else goes in it. I don't want to be like the nine lepers in Mark 17:11–19 who Jesus healed and didn't thank him. Only one of the healed lepers came back to thank him and give glory to God.

> Enter His gates with thanksgiving and his courts with praise. Give thanks to Him and praise His name.
>
> Psalm 100:4

> Don't worry about anything, but in everything, through prayer and petition with thanksgiving, let your requests be made known to God. And the peace of God, which surpasses every thought, will guard your hearts and your minds in Christ Jesus.
>
> Philippians 4:6–7

*A thought to ponder*: What do you need to thank Jesus for today?

## Backbone

I love our preacher, Michael. He preaches from the Word exactly like it says. He approaches topics that I've never heard preached from the pulpit before. He isn't afraid nor does he shy away. He approaches the topic straight out of the Bible, not from his opinion. I believe the Bible is true, every word of it. There are many accepted practices in our culture today that according to the Bible are sin. When he first started doing this, I would be nervous about what he was going to say. For example, if he was going to preach on divorce, I would have at least one friend in the congregation who had been divorced. Then there was the series on the Holy Spirit. I've never before heard the Holy Spirit preached on in a Baptist church. After attending the length of time we have, I don't get nervous anymore. He compiles all the facts from Scripture and then puts it together with the culture today. He calls *black* black or *white* white. He isn't offensive to anyone because he is using only what God said about the subject. If a person was going to be upset, they would have to be upset with God, not Michael. Today it seems like most people in general, let alone preachers, won't take a stand for what's right according to the Bible. Culture becomes the standard today for what is acceptable, instead of the Bible being the ruler.

As believers in Christ, we are free and set free from the law. Christ came not to abolish the law but to fulfill the law.

> Don't assume that I came to destroy the Law or the Prophets. I did not come to destroy but to fulfill. For I assure you: Until heaven and earth pass away, not the smallest letter or one stroke of a letter will pass from the law until all things are accomplished. Therefore, whoever breaks one of the least of these commandments and teaches people to do so will be called least in the kingdom of heaven. But whoever practices and teaches these commandments will be called great in the kingdom of heaven. For I tell you, unless your righteousness surpasses that of the scribes and Pharisees, you will never enter the kingdom of heaven.
>
> Matthew 5:17–20

*A thought to ponder*: We live under grace given through the blood of Jesus. The Holy Spirit guides us through our conscience and through the reading of the Word. We are free, free to live under God's grace, free to live morally as outlined in the Scripture.

## Tote Bags

I love tote bags. I take one with me in the car every time I leave the house. Yes, this is in addition to my purse. I am a bit of a pack rat. Before I had my Nook, I also took a tote bag of books. When we'd go on vacation, it was a lot of stuff. I now have an entire library in my purse on that one small device, so that eliminated one bag! I love tote bags for their functionality, but if I find an extra cute one, I cannot stop myself from buying it. The good thing is that I do use them—all of them. My sister gave me an extra cute one for my birthday. It is one of life's small pleasure's that make me happy. I am also happy to share them if I know someone that loves one of them. So what goes in all of these totes? Some or all of the following: my computer, a glass of tea, protein bars, journals, notebooks, pens, paper clips, stapler, more small bags with small stuff in them, a sweater, hand cream, address book, stationary, cords for my computer, Nook, and phone. This is my must-have-with-me tote bag. Then of course, there are the many other places I go that I need to tote things to. I have some in black and pink with our Pink Apostle logo on them for our ministry events. I have tote bags for my books to take to book signings. I can go on and on. I know you want me to—joking! What's the point of the tote bags? I was thinking of all these different purposes for them and how many I have and how many I use. The contents are so varied but so necessary, depending on where I am going.

I am slogging my tote bags everywhere I go, having so many to get all of my contents packed up that I need. I have my Nook to take tons of books with me everywhere. I never know when I may need what is inside one of them. Isn't it amazing that there is one book that has the answer to every question we will ever have in this life? Only one book which contains all of this? The Bible, written over two thousand years ago, is as relevant and important for our lives today as it was when it was written. It is as current and as up to date. There isn't a shelf life on it. It has sold more books than any in history and has been read more than any one other book. It's just one, packed full of more wisdom than a thousand books on psychology, love, wisdom, parenting, death, marriage, and peace.

> Oh, the depth of the riches both of the wisdom and the knowledge of God! How unsearchable His judgments and untraceable His ways! For who has known the mind of the Lord? Or who has been His counselor? Or who has ever first given to Him, and has to be repaid? For from Him and through Him and to Him are all things. To Him be the glory forever. Amen.
>
> Romans 11:33–36

*A thought to ponder*: Are you taking advantage of all the wisdom packed in this one book? At our fingertips are words of life and love. It's the perfect mystery, romance, and comedy all rolled into one!

## Umbrellas

I really like umbrellas. I keep one in my car, just in case we have a pop-up rainstorm. We once took a vacation to Disney World, and I carried an umbrella around the entire time because we had a bit of a sprinkle. I used to make my girls take umbrellas with them when they left the house and it looked like rain. They never used them. They only took them under force. They would arrive back home later, wet. I would ask them why they didn't use their umbrellas, and they would look at me and shrug. I guess it wasn't cool to stay dry. I would tell them the umbrellas would only work if they opened it and carried it around over their head.

The Word of God is the same way. It will protect us from all kinds of rain, hidden danger, and fear. We have to open it and read it to know what our protection is and then pray and ask God for his protection. It isn't automatic. If we don't do our part, he won't do his. Just like the umbrella won't open by itself, your Bible won't either.

> The one who lives under the protection of the Most High dwells in the shadow of the Almighty.
>
> Psalm 91:1

# All Creatures Great and Small

## Trust

As I am writing this, it is winter; and birds are all the rage in fashion. I had purchased a purse, a keychain, and checks with birds on them before I found this out. I thought the birds were cute and reminded me of spring. I enjoy surrounding myself with happy things, especially in the dead of winter. It seems like everyplace I turn, I am looking at birds on something. I can hear them singing in my head and see them flitting about my spring flowers in the imagination of my mind. I also like the carefree attitude of the birds. They don't worry about what they will eat or where they will sleep. They just fly around doing the thing God created them to do, without a worry in the world.

I ponder: how wonderful to go through my day, every day, without a care in the world. To trust God so much that I only concern myself with doing *my thing* daily he created me to do. To trust him so completely that a worry doesn't even begin to enter my mind. To worry is to be anxious or agitated. I've never seen a bird fly around looking anxious or agitated. In my mind, I know God is able to completely take care of me, my family, and all my problems. I want to keep a bird in some form in front of me to remind me of this.

> Aren't five sparrows sold for two pennies? Yet not one of them is forgotten in God's sight.
>
> Luke 12:6

> When I am afraid, I will trust in you. In God, whose word I praise, in God I trust; I will not fear. What can man do to me? You yourself have recorded my wanderings. Put my tears in your bottle. Are they not in your records? In God, whose word I praise, in the LORD whose word I praise, in God I trust, I will not fear.
>
> Psalm 56:3, 4, 8, 10, 11

*A thought to ponder*: What do you look at that immediately reminds you of God's faithfulness?

## Precious Treasure

My then very young grandson, Blake, expressed with great joy, "My found it! My found my Bronco!" Then with an angry expression, he added, "In there!"—pointing to the large trash bag he pulled it from. Blake's mother had been sorting through his toys to make room for his new birthday toys. He had just had his second birthday. The new toys added in to the old ones would take up too much room. This was convenient for me, as I was needing some trucks and tractors for him to play with at my house. This explains why the Bronco, one of his treasured old toys, had ended up in the trash bag. He wasn't supposed to find it until he saw it at my house.

As Blake found his beloved Bronco in the perishable container of a trash bag, I ponder on how, as believers, we have a precious treasure in a perishable container. As the Scripture says in 2 Corinthians 4:6–7, "For God who said, 'Let light shine out of darkness,' has shone in our hearts to give the light of the knowledge of God's glory in the face of Jesus Christ. Now we have this treasure in clay jars, so that this extraordinary power may be from God and not from us."

Blake didn't know what the trash bag was called, but he knew what its purpose was. He knew that his toy didn't belong in it. For him to enjoy the Bronco, he had to remove it from the trash bag and play with it. The Holy Spirit has permanent residence inside us as believers, but let's not keep him hidden there. Let's allow others to see that our strength, hope, and power is through Him who lives inside these earthen vessels. Sisters, let's bless the people we come into contact with in our day in and day out lives. Allow him to flow forth from every pour of your body, spilling out onto those who come into your space. As we focus on eternity, instead of this life, we can remember that 2 Corinthians 4:18 says, "So we do not focus on what is seen, but on what is unseen. For what is seen is temporary, but what is unseen is eternal."

*A thought to ponder*: What area of your life is God asking you to spill forth your precious treasure?

## Sophie's Bad Ear

Our beautiful Lab, Sophie, has had a bad ear her entire life. There's no reason for it. It just is. It's her right ear. I have to clean it a lot and put ointment in it. Her left ear is always fine. If I forget to doctor it, she starts digging at it and scratching it. It's a chronic problem, not a really big deal, but nonetheless, it's always ever present. After cleaning her ear for the millionth time, I began pondering on this.

In 2 Corinthians 12:7, Paul says, "So that I would not exalt myself, a thorn in the flesh was given to me." I have often wondered what this thorn was. It could have been a physical, emotional, or cultural ailment, among other things. The point is that his thorn kept him dependant on God.

Throughout our life long journey of walking with the Lord, on a consistent basis we are confronted with thorns of various types we have to continually surrender to him. More often than not, we receive victory. Sometimes the victory comes quickly, sometimes not. I also think it's common that most of us have that one thorn, that one ailment of some type that we can't rid ourselves of. It could be physical, or it could be something from our past that's very difficult to live with. Whatever your thorn is, let its purpose serve to keep you running to Christ's arms. Paul's thorn was to keep him from becoming prideful. God wants his children to be dependent on him, no matter what the circumstance. We read in Acts 7:49 that heaven is God's throne and earth is his footstool. He created and cares for everything and everyone.

*A thought to ponder*: What is your thorn, and are you living with it under God's grace?

## The Hiding Place

We had a most incredible late-spring storm. It began during the early evening, fully displaying all the majesty and power of God. More brilliant than fireworks on the Fourth of July, the light show danced on the big black night screen of the sky. The show was complete with loud and distant rumblings of thunder, followed by buckets of rain. The next morning, as I went out to survey the damage, I began picking up broken twigs and debris from the flowerbeds. The next mess to tend to was the deck. Beach towels, swimming suits, pool toys and floats were all over the place. If not for the rail around the entire deck, I would have been in the woods looking for all of this!

Our hammock is in a free-standing frame, which is screwed to the deck (because we got tired of dragging it out of the pool). I always unhook one of the ends when a storm is coming. If I don't, it looks like a sail. The wind nearly blows it away, along with the decking it is screwed to. I had everything else put back in place, so I headed over to the hammock to hook it back up. When I picked it up and unfolded it where the wind had thrown it together, I disturbed a tiny frog who had evidently gone there for cover. Instead of hopping off, it lay as still as still could be. I shook the hammock slightly, trying to get him to hop away, but he didn't budge. He had been there all night throughout that long loud storm, hiding from the elements. He had put all of his faith in the protection of that very wet hammock and wasn't ready to relinquish his hiding place yet.

> Be gracious to me, God, be gracious to me, for I take refuge in You. I will seek refuge in the shadow of Your wings until danger passes.
>
> Psalm 57:1

Just as the tiny frog took his shelter in the hiding place of the heavy wet hammock, we can take our shelter in the shadow of God's wings. As Psalm 57:1 says, we can seek refuge there until danger passes. God will never shake us out or give us a time limit to stay there. Sister, when the cares of this world become too much, tuck yourself in under his mighty wings. Therein lies safety; therein lies shelter.

*A thought to ponder*: What life's storm are you battling right now that you need to run into the shelter of God's wings?

## Always My Protector

I have walked a path where we live in the country for years. Our chocolate Lab, Maggie, walked it with me every time I went. I never had to leash her. My husband, Gene, had taught her over several months not to leave the yard. She never left our property unless I took off on my bike or by foot. Maggie would watch to see if I was turning to go home or continuing on. If I turned to go home, she would run and go home with me, without me even telling her to. She spent her days lying on the back deck, watching me or the girls through the atrium window, guarding us. Maggie was as faithful and loving as a dog could be. She died at a ripe old age of fifteen, which is a lifespan practically unheard of for a Labrador retriever.

Two very sad, lonely weeks had gone by when we adopted Sophie, a one-year old chocolate Lab, from a pound three hours from us. It wasn't long, and we loved Sophie as much as Maggie. Sophie's lifework became that of protecting me, with the same intensity of Maggie. Not having the time to work with Sophie the many hours Gene had spent with Maggie, he dug in a shock fence around our entire woods to keep her on the property. She was roaming a little, causing our two small dogs to roam off with her. The shock collar worked out great. When the weather was nice enough for her to stay outside when I'd leave for the day, it kept her from roaming. It was great piece of mind. She always tried to follow my car but stayed away from the warning zone of the shock fence. She treated it with the respect it deserved.

Every now and again, I tried taking Sophie on one of my walks with her leash, vowing each time I would never try it again. She always ended up walking me, and my shoulder would be nearly dislocated. The excitement of it absolutely overtook her! A long section of time would pass by, and I would forget and try it again. I decided the last time was really the last time. I could not get her to calm down and walk nicely with me. I had all of Sophie's dragging me around I could take.

The week following the *really last time*, I took off again, leaving Sophie in the yard with her shock collar on. My normal routine was to put her in her crate, but this particular autumn morning, the weather was spectacular, so I let her stay outside. I had no more than rounded the first curve and, within seconds, Sophie was running past me. I called her to me to check that her collar was still on, and sure enough, it was. My first thought was to go back home and crate her. My second thought was to go ahead with my walk and see what she'd do. I wasn't willing to take the chance before for fear of her running out to the highway or being hit by a car on the street. I was more concerned about her safety than to take her with me for protection. After what she endured to be with me, I decided she had earned her chance. Prove herself, she did. I was drop jawed, utterly amazed, watching her. It was like Maggie had somehow trained her. I was watching a carbon copy unfold before my eyes. Instead of the crazed dog on a leash, she never left my side. She had resumed her protector role. By the way, I held the shock collar in my hand so Sophie wouldn't get shocked going back in the yard. I forgot about it as I was walking along back down the drive. I assure you, it was working!

Sophie was so determined to get to me, enduring the shock of crossing the fence line, because of her unfailing, completely committed devotion and love for me. This reminds me of Christ's love for us.

> God's love was revealed among us in this way: God sent his one and only Son into the world so that we might live through him. Love consists

> in this: not that we loved God, but that he loved us and sent his Son to be the propitiation of our sins.
>
> 1 John 4:9–10 (HCS)

In fact, the only reason we are able to love is because, according to verse 10, "We love because he first loved us." Sophie endured a shock to be with me, but Christ endured the cross so that we could live with him for all of eternity. Sophie couldn't choose to come and live with Gene and I. We choose her from the pound to come and live with us. In the same way, we must choose Jesus Christ for our one and only personal Savior in order to have all the benefits the Bible talks about. When we have given our life to Jesus Christ, he immediately becomes our Lord and Savior. He then is our protector, among many, many other things. He becomes our everything!

> In all these things we are more than victorious through him who loved us. For I am persuaded that neither death nor life, nor angels nor rulers, nor things present, nor things to come, nor powers, nor height, nor depth, nor any other created thing will have the power to separate us from the love of God that is in Christ Jesus our Lord!
>
> Romans 8:37–39 (HCS)

*A thought to ponder*: Make Jesus Christ the Lord of your life today, and step into a life of pure, untainted love and protection. You are always on His mind!

## The Mattress

When I was four years old, Mom had gone shopping and brought my two brothers and myself a special surprise. She had purchased all of us our own book with matching record. You could play the vinyl 45 rpm record on a record player and follow along *reading* it in the book. (If you don't know what a record is, you can look it up in an encyclopedia.) I was so excited to have it. Loving books at a young age, it was my most prized possession.

My brothers and I shared a bedroom at that time. We were all only two years apart. They had bunk beds on one side of the room, and I had a twin bed on the other. I felt like my bed was the only place I had that was off limits to them. When I wanted to hide something to keep it very safe, I would slip it between my mattress and box spring when I was alone in the room. Even four-year-olds need a place to call their own personal space! This secret spot had been working very well for me. I added my book/record set to the small pile of treasures I had collected. I would slip it out when I was alone and listen to it and then slip it back. I'm sure you are guessing what happened. Yes, I went one day to sneak it out of its special spot to listen to it, and the record had gotten in the exact wrong spot and was broken. I was crushed. I was so worried about keeping it safe that it lead to my not being able to enjoy it at all. I was so afraid if I left it out with all the other books and toys that it would get lost. I was holding on to it so tightly that no one else could enjoy it, and that led to not getting to enjoy it myself. As this old childhood memory popped into my head, I began to ponder…

In this day and time, many Christians keep the good news of the gospel to ourselves. We enjoy all the benefits of being a child of the heavenly King, of having a personal relationship with Jesus Christ. We get to live in victory because He immediately forgives our every sin that we repent of. John 14:27 says Jesus gives us true peace. Ephesians 1:13–14 says when we believe on the sweet name of Jesus we are marked with a seal, a deposit guaranteeing our inheritance. According to Matthew 28:20, we don't have to fear these unsettling times we are living in because Jesus will be with us always until the very end of the age. We live in such controversial times that I think we are just plain afraid to speak out about this wonderful treasure we are harboring in our hearts. Life's great for those who have given their hearts to Christ. We need to remind ourselves that there is a big, hurting world out there full of people who don't know Jesus. Let's lift this special treasure out from under the mattress. We can't lose Him, and no matter how many people we share Him with, we can still enjoy Him all we want ourselves! Be brave, and go in love.

*A thought to ponder*: Who do you need to share the good news of Jesus Christ with?

# The Bee

During the summer when I'm taking care of our flowers, there are often many bumblebees buzzing around. To be honest, I am as scared of them as they are of me. It seems odd to me that I am afraid of something so small. When I have the water hose on the flowers where they are buzzing, I am definitely afraid they are going to come for me! It's just a good thing the water can stream over from a good distance away. I know they are as afraid that I am going to hurt them. It seems to me that it is obvious I am helping them. If the flowers die from lack of water, they'll have no nectar for their honey. I don't understand why they don't know this. Every summer, it's the same thing. They never figure out that I'm their friend. I think the little yellow and black things are so cute. If I could just somehow get a memo to them that while we are working together, we need to call a truce. I don't dare get in the middle of the beds to pull weeds while they are in the thick of it. So small that they are, they certainly cause big problems for me. Perhaps if we could both get past our fear, we could actually get a lot accomplished. My flowerbeds would be weeded and beautiful, and they wouldn't have to waste so much energy scaring me.

This is a bit humorous, albeit so true. The truth is fear can play a huge part in our lives. My husband has a fear of storms and snakes. I have a fear of heights and water. Our daughter Erin, our little Mama of our two little darlings, has a huge fear of germs. She doesn't want those babies to get sick. Our daughter Tonya has a fear of driving around semi trucks in rainy weather, stemming from an accident she was in several years ago. People are afraid of all sorts of things.

No one is really fearless. Many of our fears have been passed down to us by our parents. Even for a fear that is only real in our thoughts, it can be crippling. Is there any good news here? With any problem of any kind we have, the Lord Jesus is ready and waiting for us to call on His name.

> The one who lives under the protection of the Most High dwells in the shadow of the Almighty. I will say to the Lord, "My refuge and my fortress, my God, in whom I trust." He himself will deliver you from the hunter's net, from the destructive plague. He will cover you with his feathers; you will take refuge under his wings. His faithfulness will be a protective shield. You will not fear the terror of night, the arrow that flies by day.
>
> Psalm 91:1–5

*A thought to ponder*: We can get into many situations where it is a good thing to feel some fear. We do need to be cautious around snakes and while driving near large trucks. I have to say, the height and water thing is in my mind. No matter if our fears are real or imagined, they are problems to us. We need to remember that our God is bigger, and we can't let a fear stop us from following his will for our lives. He will carry us through. We simply pry open our hand that is so tightly gripping that fear; allowing God to take it from us. We do nothing but believe. He is our totally awesome, fearless God!

## For Such a Time as This

My Jack Russell terrier, Jackson, likes to eat. When we have guests, he jumps in their car if he gets half a chance. His goal in life is to find food. Jackson can jump onto my kitchen counter like a cat. Don't look away from your plate of food either. He'll snatch your food right out from under you! No need to vacuum often since he's already licked up all the crumbs of food. He's a better mouser than a cat. If you give him a ball, you've sealed your fate for the night. He will actually push the ball in your hand if you stop throwing it. My husband will take the ball from him when we go to bed and put it in a drawer so we can sleep, and Jackson will stare at the drawer for hours. When he smells a mole in the yard, he can have a hole dug for his entire body to fit into in a matter of seconds. Jackson is definitely focused. God made him this way. It is his purpose.

We make plans for our life. We make career goals and life goals and then make it our purpose to fulfill them. Do we stop to ask God if our goals are the goals he planned for us? I had a career with big goals that I had planned to work at until I retired. I had already accomplished a lot and was on a fast track to bigger and better success. Throughout the course of a year, God had changed my plans. I resigned, making my new life's work to found a women's ministry he led me into. Then a writing career I had never imagined I would have, which is immensely fun.

> Perhaps you have come to the kingdom for such a time as this.
>
> Esther 4:14

*A thought to ponder*: Have you asked God what he has appointed for you to do in such a time as this? He has a purpose for your life, one that he ordained before the beginning of time.

## Springtime

Ah, spring is in the air! Flowerbeds, mulch, leaves back on the trees, moles, and Jackson, our Jack Russell terrier, digging. Jackson can smell a mole in our yard and have a hole dug big enough for his entire body to fit into in two seconds flat. He will also go after a snake, and he's a better mouser than any cat ever was. This was never much of a problem, until a tiny little mouse decided to live in one of my flowerbeds. It is the bed directly attached to the carport, which is attached to the house; so it's very visible. And it was beautiful, I might add, when spring arrived. It had never been more beautiful, until Jackson smelled the mouse. I couldn't figure out why he had destroyed that flowerbed. He had never dug up a flowerbed before. Sure, he's dug tons of holes in the yard, mostly on the border by the woods, hunting those little moles. He's eight years old and has never done any real damage. I bought a new large flower, moved more around, and filled in the holes until it looked as good as new. My dilemma is what to do with the mouse. Gene saw it first; then I saw him scampering across the edge of the deck, running to safety. I hate mice and normally would have already had Gene set a trap. But when I saw it, he was so small and tiny. I thought if he stayed outside, what harm could he do? Gene thinks he's eating one of the small pieces of the dogs' food I drop for his daily portion of food. I keep it in the carport in a tub. I can see the little mouse trying to carry that one ball of food in his hands to safety. It would look like me trying to carry a boulder.

As the mouse was the problem of my torn-up flowerbeds, but he was hidden, so goes it with us. Psalm 19:12 says, "Who perceives his unintentional sins? Cleanse me from my hidden faults." Matthew 10:26 says, "There is nothing covered that won't be uncovered, and nothing hidden that won't be made known."

*A thought to ponder*: I had to find out what the hidden problem was in the flowerbed, but God sees all of our hidden sin. He doesn't have to go on a hunt to find it. Sin in our life breaks our fellowship with him. Confess it. He already knows about it. He is faithful and just to cleanse us from all unrighteousness when we do!

# Letting Go

## On the Guadalupe

Several years ago, my husband and I took a road trip to Galveston, Texas, working our way up to Dallas, Texas. As we were working our way up the state, Gene decided he wanted us to canoe the Guadalupe River. I am really no fun to do any type of sports activity with. I'm not athletic at all, and I don't enjoy participating either. My idea of enjoying the beautiful outdoors is reading a book in the shade while sipping a large glass of iced tea. Of course, dining with a friend at a restaurant on an outside patio counts too. I love to ride my big cruiser bike (is that a sport?) and drive my convertible with the top down. That's about it. Are you getting the picture? That canoe trip on the Guadalupe was the first and last time I have or ever will canoe.

I wanted to be a good sport, so I agreed. I thought, how hard could it be? Did I mention I can't swim? Or that I'm afraid of water that is deeper than my four-foot swimming pool? Texas was having a drought that year, and the river was very low, which was how Gene sold me on it. So off we went with our rented canoe into the calm, shallow, peaceful waters. We both had an oar, and I was getting the hang of it pretty quickly. The woods the river ran through were very beautiful and calming. Well, they were calming until I realized I hadn't seen anything but trees and water for a long time and could see nothing else as far as I could see. Very beautiful, but claustrophobia was setting in. I took both oars and began to paddle as quickly as I could. Gene kept telling me to relax and enjoy floating along, but I was panicking with all the tranquility and paddled faster and faster. He was laughing at me the entire time, relaxing while I was rowing my arms off. By the time we arrived at our next destination a few hours later, Gene had to find me a hotel room with a whirlpool bathtub. My muscles were feeling like a load of bricks. It was all I could do to walk to the room. It took a good long soak with bubbles and lots of heat before I could finally move again.

I was reading in my Bible in Exodus about how the Israelites left Egypt, with Pharaoh and his army pursuing them. They were afraid and Moses told them in 14:14, "The Lord will fight for you; you need only to be still" (NLT). Fight for them he did! While the Israelites crossed the Red Sea on dry ground, the Red Sea swallowed up the Egyptians, drowning every one of them. God protected and saved them, all by himself. While rowing on the Guadalupe, Gene was *still* and enjoyed the moment, while I, on the other hand, was fighting with all my might to get back to civilization. Gene was rested, and I was so sore I couldn't move.

Don't we do this with God? He still wants to fight our battles for us. We try to help him, but he doesn't need our help. He only needs us to let go and give the situation to him and be still. He is the same God today who dried up the Red Sea so many, many years ago. He hasn't lost any of his mighty power. His yoke is easy and his burden is light. This is where we find rest for our souls. Sister, be still in him and find peace.

*A thought to ponder*: What battle are you fighting that you need to turn over to God?

## Research

I am one of those who are faithful brand followers, having had an item that worked well. I also like to match *everything*. I have made two buying mistakes this way. I had a convection microwave oven that I absolutely loved, easy to use, and used often for baked goods. It had broken, and my husband wanted me to purchase a new one right away. I wanted to wait because my stove was getting old, knowing it would only be a matter of time before it went out. I decided to purchase the new convection oven when I purchased the new stove—of course, so they would match. A few years later, that's exactly what I did. I had done a lot of researching for my new stove. I had it picked out long before I needed it. Without researching how the convection microwave oven worked in this same brand, I purchased it assuming it would be great like the stove I loved. Big boo-boo! I have had it three years and am just now starting to get the hang of it. I still can't make it work like my old one. The old one, albeit a different brand, was much easier to use.

My other buying mistake I made by assuming all items are equal within the same brand was replacing my tired worn out serger sewing machine. Again, instead of repurchasing the same one I had worn out that had worked so well, I went and bought another in the same brand of my regular sewing machine I loved. I didn't research this either. I loved the sewing machine so much, it never occurred to me that the serger wouldn't work out the same. Five years later, after great aggravation, I traded it in on a different brand.

As I pondered on this, I need to remember that simply because I love the way an item works doesn't automatically mean all other products in the same brand will perform the same way. I can't assume this. I have to compare, ask questions, and do research on each product. It takes a considerable amount of time to do this on the front end but saves so much time after the purchase.

To some degree we do this in many aspects of our lives. Even in our Christian circles, within our churches, we want to *match*. Some won't step inside the doors of a church because of the name, like a brand, on the sign, while others will only go to a church that has that one particular name on it. Instead of doing our research and checking a matter out, many times instead we simply assume something from the past, which actually has absolutely nothing to do with it today in one way or another. If our friends, whom we want to *match*, have an opinion about something, many times we take it on as our own without looking into it. We can be missing out on a great journey God has for our life or on a blessing by not asking questions and doing our own research.

Through the guidance of the Holy Spirit and prayer, Luke 11:9–10 says,

> "Keep asking, and it will be given to you. Keep searching, and you will find. Keep knocking, and the door will be opened to you. For everyone who asks receives, and the one who searches finds, and to the one who knocks, the door will be opened."

*A thought to ponder*: Lord, what circumstance in my life right now am I not looking at correctly?

## Cast-Iron Fittings

At the time I am writing this, my husband and I have run a commercial plumbing business a little over nine years. We originally leased an office/warehouse, then built and owned one, then sold it, and are preparing to move back into a lease. It's time to downsize the warehouse and get things in order, so when Gene's ready to retire, he can. So the business of downsizing the warehouse is a bit difficult because Gene never wants to get rid of anything. Jeff, our warehouse manager, was showing me some of the things that came with the purchase of the business that we have never and will never use. One of these items is a huge pallet of very large and heavy cast-iron fittings. I don't know how much Jeff will be able to talk Gene into letting him scrap—well, good luck with that, Jeff! Gene would rather pack up and drag the fittings, along with all the other virtually useless stuff out there, because "ya never know when some day ya might need it!" And he reminds me, there have been a (very) few times in the nine-plus years we have been in business that he has needed one of those dinosaurs that you can't even buy now. I have a feeling that, for the third time, we will be dragging all of our stuff—the useful and the useless—with us, once again.

I began to ponder on this. I also keep a good amount of personal stuff in our home. I like to call them my collections, and I do collect a variety of things like cookbooks, shoes, purses…oh well, we are two birds of a feather, Gene and I. I pondered how as we like to keep our material baggage, how much more do we many times keep emotional baggage? Jesus said,

> Come to me, all you who are weary and burdened, and I will give you rest. All of you, take up my yoke and learn from me, because I am gentle and humble in heart, and you will find rest for yourselves. For my yoke is easy and my burden is light.
>
> Matthew 11:28–30

Sisters, one thing I have learned is this: we can't keep dragging around all of our "stuff" on our shoulders. They just aren't big or strong enough to hold up under it. Oh! What freedom and joy when we truly hand over those heavy bags to our Redeemer! What a weight lifted off! After we have really passed it from our tight fist to his open hand we feel as light as a feather and our peace and joy returns to us. Gone not only is the baggage, but the worry, the stress, and the heavy heart. Lord Jesus, what freedom we have when we trust in you, our faithful God!

*A thought to ponder*: Are you carrying around emotional baggage? If so, pray and release it to Jesus!

## Random Thoughts

You know how you wonder about random things from time to time? One of my random thoughts is if you only had a few moments to save anything from your house, what would it be? This thought floated through my mind from time to time, never getting an answer. I thought it would be pictures and the fire lock box holding our important documents, among other things.

Often, we don't really know how we will respond to an emergency situation until we are in it. Our grandchildren, five and three years old at the time, were spending the night with us when a friend woke us up with a phone call at 4:00 a.m. with news that a tornado was on the ground just a few miles from our house. We don't have a basement, so I rushed to prepare the bathtub to lay the kids in. Next I ran and picked up Addi and Blake out of their bed, getting them situated in the safe spot as quickly as possible. So they wouldn't be scared, I told them we were playing campout. Gene grabbed the weather radio and the dogs, and we were bracing ourselves to be hit any minute. As soon as we were situated, Gene realized neither one of us had a pair of shoes on. I ran out of the bathroom to grab us both a pair. It was scary out of the bathroom. For the first time since the phone call, the question ran through my mind, "While I'm out here, shouldn't I be grabbing some stuff"? The answer was no. I found Gene and I a pair of shoes, and I grabbed my purse because my car key was in it. I was hoping if we were hit, the car would still be outside so we could drive to our daughter and son-in-law's house. I was wearing my pajamas and an old sweatshirt. While I was hunting the shoes, I ran through that proverbial list in my mind. Pictures? No. Lock box? No. Clothes? Jewelry? No no no no. All that mattered to me that was in my house at that very moment in time was in my bathroom: Gene, Addi, Blake, and the dogs. Nothing else mattered. It was all stuff that could be replaced and certainly wasn't important. I had all the memories of the pictures in my mind, and I just didn't care about anything else.

The bathroom door began to vibrate, and I was preparing to throw myself on top of the kids along with pillows and a quilt. The tornado missed us, hitting neighbors and a street down the road. A neighboring town was hit very hard, killing six and leaving many homeless, taking with it many businesses and even their hospital.

> Lord, reveal to me the end of my life and the number of my days. Let me know how short-lived I am. You, indeed, have made my days short in length, and my life span as nothing in your sight. Yes, every mortal man is only a vapor. Certainly, man walks about like a mere shadow. Indeed, they frantically rush around in vain, gathering possessions without knowing

> who will get them. Now, Lord, what do I wait for? My hope is in you.
>
> Psalm 39:4–7

No one knows how many days we have on this earth. Some people think they will "make their peace with God" on their deathbed. Some of us won't have a deathbed. The tornado hit the nearby town so fast the town siren didn't go off until after it had hit. Most of the people were in their beds asleep. For sure, they didn't have time to do anything, let alone pray.

*A thought to ponder*: All we can take with us on this earth into the next life is people. Re-evaluate where you are spending your time each day. Are you putting countless energy into gathering possessions, without even knowing who will get them when you are gone? Or are you putting your time into people?

## Oblivious

My then sixteen-month-old grandson, Blake, was playing at my house with then his three-year-old sister, Addi. I raised two girls, so I am still getting used to how little boys operate. He is very focused and fast, and from time to time, he does get away from me! This particular day, spring had arrived, and it was so good to finally be able to play outside. After lunch, the kids wanted to play on the front porch while I was finishing the cleanup. Addi is very good at helping me keep a close eye on Blake. I didn't think any harm could be done, so I told them yes. About the third time I went to check on them, he was gone. My heart leaped into my chest, and then Addi told me he was fine. He had just gone around the corner into the carport. I ran to get him (we live in the country—in case you think I had lost my last marble), and he was happily pushing his little umbrella stroller, as he often did, with his rocks, cars, and tractors in it. I was relieved to see he was fine but simultaneously horrified to see that a screw on the side of the stroller was scratching a line all the way down my new black Sebring. (Erin, don't worry—I told Dad he couldn't tell you because it was my fault he got away from me!!!) After the shock wore off, I got to pondering on this.

It was amazing to me that he was completely oblivious that this was happening. But he was, however, only a baby and had absolutely no idea that anything was wrong. I pondered on how we are like this many times in our own lives. When we aren't staying in the Word, getting to know the character of God, and praying for direction for our lives, I think many times God is in heaven watching us, shaking his head, and saying to himself, "They don't even know they are messing up! If only they would look in the Book!" How many times have we "scratched the paint off on our brand new car" and didn't even know it? How many times have we veered off in the wrong direction, totally oblivious that we have, missing a huge blessing God had for us? Blake wasn't old enough to know anything was wrong. We are old enough to know that we have to keep our eyes on Christ for our road map to our life. He is anxiously waiting for us to ask him what it is we are to do, and by spending time with him, the Holy Spirit will lead and guide us.

I had my body-shop man buff the scratch out as well as he could without repainting the door. He did a great job. There are only about eighteen inches that didn't come completely out, and it is very difficult to see. I will never have it fixed better because it is a reminder for me to keep my eyes on Christ, the author and finisher of my faith, and to not drift through life oblivious to the work he has for me to do, that which he prepared for me before time began. This is where true happiness lies—when we are fulfilling the call God has placed on our life, walking in his will.

> For we are his creation—created in Christ Jesus for good works, which God prepared ahead of time so that we should walk in them.
>
> Ephesians 2:10

> For I know the plans I have for you- this is the Lord's declaration—plans for your welfare, not for disaster, to give you a future and a hope.
>
> Jeremiah 29:11

*A thought to ponder*: Let's let go of our own plans, and give God complete control of our lives. When it's all said and done, I'm sure we will see his was definitely the better way!

## My Orchestrated Day

I love to make lists, schedules, plans. And I hate when my planned schedule changes! At the same time, however, I pray every morning for God to orchestrate my day and be in control of everything I say and do.

Once I make arrangements for any type of training or ministry seminar, I go—no matter what, even if I end up going alone. I am a Beth Moore fan. I love her because she is an awesome anointed Bible teacher, funny, real, and leads her students to dig deeply into the word of God. I have had plans to attend one of her conferences for six months—registration, hotel, and friends going all lined up. This week I did the unthinkable: I broke one of my rules. I canceled out just a few days before we were to go. Like everyone else, my schedule is crazy. Crazy doing lots of good things, but crazy nonetheless. Sometimes it just gets plain out of control. I got to thinking if I stayed home, I would have an entire *extra* day to get more things done before the next Saturday when I was hosting a surprise birthday party for my mom. I decided I needed to rearrange and straighten this very large closet I have, which, by the way, no one would ever see. It is against my personality to actually rest or take it easy. Next came the most difficult part. Explaining to the other girls why I wasn't going—a difficult task for me since the only time I let myself off the hook with anything would be a death or hospitalization. Ringing a bell with anyone???? The bottom line was I knew I just wasn't supposed to go this time.

So this was how it turned out. A few days before I would have left, I messed up the bottom of my back. After visiting the chiropractor and my massage therapist, it was better, but I was moving at the speed of a snail for the first few hours I was up until the muscles got warmed up and loosened again. I wouldn't have even been able to climb the auditorium stairs to get to my seat. Instead of spending the day killing myself cleaning out that huge closet, I actually had a very relaxing, enjoyable day (since I had no choice).

As I pondered this, I thought what in the world does God have to do to get me to rest? The Holy Spirit is housed in the bodies of believers, and God commanded us to take care of them.

> Do you not know that your body is a temple of the Holy Spirit, who is in you, whom you have received from God? You are not your own; you were bought at a price. Therefore honor God with your body.
>
> 1 Corinthians 6:19 & 20 (NIV)

My day looked like this, my day that I asked God to orchestrate. First, I had a massage, then a leisurely visit to one of my very favorite shops and good chat with the owner who is a friend, ate lunch with my husband, surfed the net a bit, typed a pondering, watched an old favorite show, and actually took a nap! I felt much more rested, and my back had relaxed a bit more. I think sometimes we wear our business like a badge and feel embarrassed when we rest. It feels like we are being lazy. The reality is that in order to take good care of our bodies, we do need to stop from our daily business from time to time. It's not only good for our physical body; we are much more effective mentally in our work and ministries when we take a break.

*A thought to ponder*: Let's remember to not only pray for God to orchestrate our day, but to let him be in charge when he wants to change our well made plans. Even rest can be an act of worship unto God. Rest well!

## Pure and Simple

I love how small children tell it pure and simple. They don't make things up; they just tell it like it is. As soon as our granddaughter could barely sit on a stool, Papa Gene had her "working" beside him. He would be at his drafting table doing estimates with blueprints with his working ruler, and Addi would be using the broken ruler on her side of the prints. Papa would be making straight lines in all different colors, while Addi made different colored circles all over her end. I only asked him to keep her from falling off the stool. This ruler they used cost about seventy-five dollars. Not a fortune, but enough to be careful with the tool. Little Addi bounced off to play something else for a while, and Papa realized she'd taken off with the working ruler. He called her into his office and asked her where it was. After being deep in thought for at least three seconds, which would max out an eighteen-month-old's brain, she said, "I lost it, Papa."

She then turned and ran back off to play. This sent Gene, her mother, Erin, and me into hysterical laughter. She was as serious as serious could be. It didn't enter her mind to make up excuses. No, she told it straight out. No sugarcoating, just the facts.

Addi and Blake's parents, Erin and Jacob, went through the licensing process to foster to adopt. They have put Blake's outgrown toddler bed upstairs in the playroom. They won't leave it there, but they have to have a bed ready and waiting. Since they have no idea when or if this will ever happen, this spot works for now. Blake was giving the reason for the bed in the playroom to his great-grandmothers. He said, "It's for adoption. If we get a call, we get a baby. If we don't get a call, we don't get a baby." And that was that. It could never have been explained any simpler.

Two wonderful examples of Psalm 24. This is what clean hands and a pure heart look like.

> The one who has clean hands and a pure heart, who has not set his mind on what is false, and who has not sworn deceitfully. He will receive a blessing from the Lord, and righteousness from the God of his salvation.
>
> Psalm 24:4–5

*A thought to ponder*: As adults, we often find ourselves in challenging situations and feel that there is no simple way out. But if we wade through all the junk, it is very simple 99 percent of the time. We don't want to admit we "lost it" or take the blame for something we did. By diving into the situation like Psalm 24, with clean hands and a pure heart, it's like ripping off a Band-Aid. The sting is over with quickly by doing the right thing on the front end.

## Checks

I have always been a check writer. No cash for me. It is a fun day when it is time to pick out new checks. I like everything fun and cute. My daughters kept talking about online bill pay. What fun would that be? Not write out the checks? Just click some lines on the bank website and you're done? I don't think I can trust that. Hmmm… Finally, I looked at it. I started clicking, and then I clicked some more. It took all of ten minutes, and I was hooked. Okay, I'm slow to warm up to new ideas sometimes, I know. I entered all of the information to try it, and when I actually paid the bills, I called Erin and told her that was the laziest way ever to pay bills. I loved it! I can't believe how fast it is. Now I'm trying to switch myself over to cash for the weekly shopping. This is hard for me. I hate using cash, but I love balancing the checkbook in fifteen minutes because there are so few entries. I've been using the online bill pay now for two months, and I have to say I've substituted it permanently for the old check-writing method I have used all my life up to this point. I'm going to keep trying to get used to substituting cash for checks for all the routine weekly shopping. This is much harder for me, but I'll keep at it.

Through life, we are always substituting one thing for another. The most wonderful thing I substituted was my sin and eternal death for the cross of Christ. He gave his life for me as propitiation for my sin, and I accepted it!

> This Jesus is the stone despised by you builders, who has become the cornerstone. There is salvation in no one else, for there is no other name under heaven given to people by which we must be saved.
>
> Acts 4:11–12

*A thought to ponder*: Have you substituted your sin sick heart for the cross of Christ?

## Making Soap

My mom and I have discussed how we can both turn something that should be so simple into nothing short of a fiasco. We have a knack for adding to a simple task until we are undone. We do this with family dinners. We start with a simple menu and end up being exhausted because of all the extra items we added to the menu.

My friends have all gone wild over Pinterest, an online pin board. I'm still figuring out what it is. Lots of them are making their own cleaning products from recipes they are finding on Pinterest. I think this is interesting, although I am still somewhat skeptical. I decided to try the liquid hand soap. It only needs three ingredients, one of which is water, and, after melting on the stove, twelve hours to cool down and thicken. Doesn't seem like it's very time consuming, does it? Okay, I'm still working on my first batch. I evidently used soap that was too moisturizing to make it the right consistency. I had to remelt it and add more soap. The lady who shared her recipe uses a soap brand that I can't locate in my area. I thought I should use the one she used since I was having problems. I then spent a good bit of time on the phone calling stores hunting this soap. With no success, I went to the internet. I did find it there but decided I shouldn't leave it for a week waiting for it to come in. To be sure to waste more time and make a seemingly simple thing complicated, I began to call more stores, but success! I had a breakthrough as I stopped and went to a store five minutes from my house to purchase Ivory soap.

I tend to do this in all areas of my life. I want things to be nice, and I like being hospitable. But come on, Ruth, there needs to be some balance here! Yes, I think I am rewiring my brain to determine if this complication is necessary or not.

> Come to Me, all of you who are weary and burdened, and I will give you rest. All of you, take up My yoke and learn from Me, because I am gentle and humble in heart, and you will find rest for yourselves. For My yoke is easy and My burden is light.
>
> Matthew 11:28–30

*A thought to ponder*: Are you wearing yourself out doing things not really necessary, or have you taken on something as your responsibility that no one, including God, has asked you to? Lay it down, give it to Jesus, and find rest.

## A Dying Wish

I was visiting with an elderly lady at a grocery store this morning. Her husband died one year ago. He died on his tractor, and they aren't sure why—a heart attack, etc. She shared with me how he had told her many times that he hoped the Lord will let him die on his tractor and not in a nursing home. They were in church the day before, and she said he had prayed an extra long time that day. He didn't share with her why, but isn't this interesting? I thought, how like our God! He blesses those who are righteous on this earth, and this was a righteous, God-fearing man. Our life isn't always a bed of roses just because we belong to Christ; many times it's the opposite. But our heavenly Father loves us so much. This story absolutely touches my heart. It shows us the heart of God, the loving, caring, compassionate heart of God.

> I assure you: If you have faith and do not doubt, you will not only do what was done to the fig tree, but even if you tell this mountain, 'Be lifted up and thrown into the sea', it will be done. And if you believe, you will receive whatever you ask for in prayer.
>
> Mathew 21:21–22

*A thought to ponder*: When we aren't blessed with a loving earthly father, it can be so hard to understand the character of God. Break down the walls you have put up between you and God, and allow yourself to feel the great love he has for you.

## Hand Sanitizer

I am on the volunteer chaplain corps at our local hospital. I only minister once a month. I enjoy serving the Lord in this way very much. He led me to do this. You'll think this is funny, but before I began this service, I hate hospitals. I mean, I completely hated to be in a hospital. It's been eight months since I began this ministry, and when I go in now, I don't even think about it. I'm not sure when it happened. I don't even realize I'm in a hospital until I get in the first room, and I realize the person is sick. When we step out in faith into the path God is leading us to, he takes care of all of our little quirks and worries. I like to read a psalm to the patients while I am with them.

Like most of us, I have several Bibles. I take my red one, instead of my study Bible, because it is lighter and thinner. It makes it a little easier to handle with the clipboard. Each time I leave a room, I am to use the hand sanitizer that is hanging by the door. I'm sure the hospital's hand sanitizer is stronger and better than the kind we buy at Walgreens. The first time I used this particular Bible, I noticed red dye was getting all over my hands. I kept going until I finished with my list and then went to the bathroom to try and wash it off. My Bible had (and still has) blotchy spots on it. It actually takes the color off my Bible. It is a good leather one too. I still take it, but I am now very careful to keep it on top of the clipboard until my hands dry off.

My Bible is looking a bit strange. The leather is still in good shape, but it almost has dots on it. The inside is still in great shape too. I purchased this Bible on a clearance table at my local Christian bookstore. It was sitting there because when they engraved the name of the first person who purchased it, they messed up and put it on the back. It has this unsightly scribbled out blob where that was. It was a different translation than I used, and I had been wondering about it. That's why I purchased it in the first place. That way, if I didn't care for it, I wasn't out much money. You guessed it—it has become one of my favorites. As I said earlier, the cover is very nice leather. Now that I've read it so much, it is broken in like a pair of favorite shoes. It is so soft and supple, easy to hold with broken in pages that turn easily. Isn't that how it goes? This Bible that is getting so marred on the outside is the one I grab and want to take with me. It used to bother me about the messed-up cover, and that was when it was only the scratched-out name. I decided that I didn't care what the outside of it looks like. It's what is on the inside that counts. The inside is better than ever; marked up with favorite verses and so easy to find things I'm looking for.

> This is why I tell you: Don't worry about your life, what you will eat or what you will drink; or about your body, what you will wear. Isn't life more than food and the body more than

> clothing? Look at the birds of the sky: they don't sow or reap or gather into barns, yet your heavenly Father feeds them. Aren't you worth more than they? Can any of you add a single cubit to his height by worrying? And why do you worry about clothes? Learn how the wildflowers of the field grow: they don't labor or spin thread. Yet I tell you that not even Solomon in all his splendor was adorned like one of these! If that's how God clothes the grass of the field, which is here today and thrown into the furnace tomorrow, won't He do much more for you- you of little faith? So don't worry, saying, 'What will we eat?' or 'What will we drink?' or 'What will we wear?' For the idolaters eagerly seek all these things, and your heavenly Father knows that you need them. But seek first the kingdom of God and His righteousness, and all these things will be provided for you. Therefore don't worry about tomorrow, because tomorrow will worry about itself. Each day has enough trouble of its own.
>
> Matthew 6:25–34

*A thought to ponder*: In the same way we aren't to worry about what we eat, drink, or wear, I don't need to worry about the cover my Bible's wearing. God is so good to us. As he isn't concerned about what things look like on the outside, neither should we.

# From My Heart

## Laughter

I laugh very easily. I didn't realize it until one of my friends said to me not so long ago that one of the things she liked about me most was my gift of laughter. I never thought of laughter as a gift before. If it can be a gift, then I have it. Malicious laughter isn't who I am, but I laugh at and with everything else, including myself, a lot. I try to let go of the negative side of things quickly, knowing God has full control of my life and what's happening in it. I dump the heavy things off on his shoulders and keep mine light. Our physical bodies aren't made to carry around all of this stress and hang onto the baggage. Let it go! Hand it off to him. He is more than able to work out all the bumps that pop up in your life. There has been much research done on the health benefits of laughing. Among other things, here are a few benefits from helpguide.org.

- **Laughter relaxes the whole body.** A good, hearty laugh relieves physical tension and stress, leaving your muscles relaxed for up to 45 minutes after.

- **Laughter boosts the immune system.** Laughter decreases stress hormones and increases immune cells and infection-fighting antibodies, thus improving your resistance to disease.

- **Laughter triggers the release of endorphins,** the body's natural feel-good chemicals. Endorphins promote an overall sense of well-being and can even temporarily relieve pain.

- **Laughter protects the heart.** Laughter improves the function of blood vessels and increases blood flow, which can help protect you against a heart attack and other cardiovascular problems.

Let go, give your woes to God, and laugh! You'll feel better, and your health will improve too.

> A joyful heart is good medicine, but a broken spirit dries up the bones.
>
> Proverbs 17:22

What is the definition of joy according to the Bible?

> Then I will come to the altar of God, to God, my greatest joy. I will praise you with lyre, God, my God.
>
> Psalm 43:4

*A thought to ponder*: When is the last time you had a really good belly laugh? If you can't remember, then it's time!

## Bittersweet

You may think from a lot of the stories I write that I don't have any difficult moments. The truth is that isn't true for anyone, no matter what their life looks like. One of the bittersweet moments in my life was when my daughter Tonya moved fourteen and a half hours away from me. My head was so happy for her. She had graduated from SIU with her masters degree, gotten a great job, and was ready to begin the life she had been working so hard toward for six years. My heart wasn't happy at all. The truth is I had a very hard time getting used to her being so far away. I know there are many moms who have it much worse. I had a list I would recite of all the things that could be worse when I would get sad. I said I'm not a negative person, and I'm not. I also don't believe in coincidence. I believe Tonya and Josh are in Maryland because that is where God wants them to be for their benefit. So how can I begrudge it? I don't. However, I still have a human heart and emotions. They've been in Maryland six years now, and I'm doing much better with it. I can't say I love it that they are there, but I am really fine now. For the first several years, I had to see her by three months or I would just start crying all the time, and I'm not a crier. I can go six months now and be good, but that's the limit. I am sure many of you reading this are thinking you'd love to have my big heartache I've had to deal with. I know some of you have buried children and are waiting impatiently to see them in heaven. I have both a brother and a sister who have a child in heaven. I am sure they would trade places with me any day.

The point I wanted to make is that while we can acknowledge that things are how they should be and sometimes not, God wants us to tell him when we are hurting. He made us, and he knows what will make us sad. In fact, in telling him and crying to him is the only way to be healed. He can, will, and does heal our hearts. He makes the pain diminish. After all, he also knows what it's like to lose a child.

> In the same way the Spirit also joins to help in our weakness, because we do not know what to pray for as we should, but the Spirit Himself intercedes for us with unspoken groanings. And He who searches the hearts knows the Spirit's mind set, because He intercedes for the saints according to the will of God.
>
> Romans 8:26–27

*A thought to ponder*: Have you turned your hurts over to God? He can and will heal you!

## I'll Do It!

See if this scenario sounds familiar: I see a need to be filled. I quickly raise my hand—"I'll do it!" I see a person with a need, and I quickly take it on as my responsibility. Someone calls me with a problem, "I'll fix it," I say.

One day, I realized that just because there is a need to be filled doesn't mean it is for me to fix. Just because I see a need doesn't automatically mean I am the one to fill it. Much of what is before me, God is asking me to get involved with. If we don't see the need, we could never help. The difference is: Where I used to automatically jump in, I now ask God if this is for me. When we take things on ourselves that he isn't asking us to take on, there will be no joy in it, it will be hard, and it won't go well. When it's for us, it may be hard; but we can tell he is there guiding us and giving us strength. When we take on a need that wasn't ours to take, we stole the blessing from the person who it was intended for.

> I delight to do Your will, my God; Your instruction resides within me.
>
> Psalm 40:8

*A thought to ponder*: Don't use this as a copout to not minister at all. When we are walking in the will of God for our life, even the most difficult of circumstances works. It's part of the mystery of God. Don't miss out on your blessing by shrinking back when he's calling you out! We can never even begin to repay Christ for what he gave for us. Let's be willing to love others because of the great love he shows to us.

## Creation

The ocean calls my name when it's been to long since I've seen it. Southern Illinois is a beautiful place to live, and I admire and appreciate it every day. We don't have mountains, but we do have very big hills. The land is breathtaking. We have lots of lakes, but no ocean. The nearest ocean beach is nine hours away. Once in a while, I need to gaze on it. Once on a vacation to Florida, the ocean was very turbulent. It was rather scary looking, but it mesmerized me. I couldn't stop looking at it. I can never get over the beauty God created for us to live in.

My mind wanders about the beauty of heaven. We will see colors we have never seen, colors we don't even have names for. We will smell things the finest perfume can't hold a candle to and taste food beyond imagination. God loves beauty. He made it. I used to feel silly for liking things to look cute or pretty until the day I realized that God created it and he created me to like it. He created us all with different tastes, and we don't have to apologize for how he made us. I thank him for allowing us to live in this place of untold glory. He is so good to us.

> May His glorious name be praised forever; the whole earth is filled with His glory.
>
> Psalm 72:19

*A thought to ponder*: Allow yourself to be aware of the beauty that surrounds you the next time you step outside. Thank God for creating this for you to live amongst!

## Stuff

I like my stuff. One example is that I like purses and have a nice-sized collection of them. I change them out almost daily. I think it's fun. I like cute paper, nice pens (that are cute) and office supplies! I worried for a while about having all this stuff I have, while many don't have so much. Then one day I decided if someone says they like something I have, I'll give it to them. If I could part easily with the stuff, then it didn't own me or my heart. So this is what I did. Not always, but often—very often. I like to wear big pins on my jean jackets, and often, I'll get a compliment on the particular one I'm wearing. It is so fun to take it off and say, "Here, have it." The lady is always taken by surprise. Lately, anytime I've been out in a coffee shop writing with my Bible and computer, I have had a person mention my Bible I was using. I say "was" in the literal sense. My Bible stash is getting thin, and today I'm using one of my favorites. I have been pretty afraid that I would lose it. This one I don't want to part with. Okay, I think it's all right to keep a few things…

> Don't collect for yourselves treasures on earth, where moth and rust destroy and where thieves break in and steal. But collect for yourselves treasures in heaven, where neither moth or

> rust destroys, and where thieves don't break in and steal. For where your treasure is, there your heart will be also.
>
> Matthew 6:19–21

*A thought to ponder*: What do you have that you couldn't stand the thought of to lose? Determine if this is appropriate treasure. Is it people, or things?

## The Final Pondering

I am now writing the final pondering for this book. Surprisingly, I am glad to have it finished but also a bit sad to be done. While I have been writing it for quite sometime, the past three weeks have been dedicated to nothing else. I ask myself what motivates me to do this? What motivates me to spend so much time writing? First of all, because God places all of these thoughts in my head, and until I write them down, I have no rest. I am amazed at this thing that God has done with me, because of all the talents he has blessed me with, writing was not one. These ponderings are a complete gift from the Holy Spirit—an outpouring of all he has put into my life and my head these past fifty years. I am passionate about women's ministry. I am all about women knowing who they are in Christ and whose are they. I am passionate about women knowing how to walk through this life with victory and with joy in the Lord, no matter what life has thrown at them. I wanted you to hear my heart. I would love to hear yours. You can contact me through my website, www.ruthteal.com or my author Facebook page, Silver Linings. God has put us both here in this place in time for a reason. We don't have to do this thing alone. The basis for everything I write is to encourage you in the Lord. That is what I am crazy about. I am crazy about you, and together we'll do this thing called life together. This is one of my favorite passages:

> For this reason I bow my knees before the Father from whom every family in heaven and on earth is named. I pray that He may grant you, according to the riches of His glory, to be strengthened with power through His Spirit in the inner man, and that the Messiah may dwell in your hearts through faith. I pray that you, being rooted and firmly established in love, may be able to comprehend with all the saints what is the length and width, height and depth of God's love, and to know the Messiah's love that surpasses knowledge, so you may be filled with all the fullness of God. Now to Him who is able to do above and beyond all that we ask or think—according to the power that works in you—to Him be glory in the church and in Christ Jesus to all generations, forever and ever. Amen.
>
> Ephesians 3:14–21

*The final pondering thought*: You are living out your life right now one day at a time. You can never get today (or yesterday) back. It is gone. Are you making your life count? Are you living in the perfect will of God for your life? If you're not sure, ask him! There is no better place to be living than in the center of his will.

See you in the next book,
Ruth XO

# Afterword

It seems that many Christians today speak of salvation as something that is a past and completed event. I hear many people say, "I am saved" or "I already did that". However, a careful consideration of the teaching of salvation in Scripture reveals a much more dynamic and beautiful picture of God's plan to redeem his children. When asked if I am saved, the best answer is *yes*, *no*, and *somewhat*. As a child of God, my sins were declared forgiven by a Holy God (yes). Though a child of God, I have not fully experienced the extent of glorification that will happen when Jesus returns (no). As a child of God, I continue to experience more and more presence of God and the sanctifying work of God in my life (somewhat).

In that context, we recognize the fullness of salvation. Theologians would call this the Application of Redemption.

| | |
|---|---|
| Regeneration | Brought to Life |
| Conversion | Respond in Faith |
| Justification | Declared to be Righteous |
| Sanctification | Experiencing New Life |
| Glorification | Fully alive in Body and Spirit |

**Regeneration:** an unseen and miraculous act of God in which he imparts new spiritual life.

**Conversion:** our willing response to the gospel, in which we genuinely confess, "Jesus is Lord" and believe "He has been raised."

**Justification:** an instantaneous and legal act of God in which he considers our sins forgiven and Christ's righteousness as belonging to us, and declares us righteous in his sight.

**Sanctification**: a progressive partnering with God in which we become more like Christ in attitude and action.

**Glorification**: when Christ returns and gives all believers of all time, at the same time, perfect resurrection bodies like his own.

Michael Nave,
Lead Pastor, Cornerstone Church, Marion, Illinois